Introduction to British Constitutional

Introduction to British Constitutional Law

Sixth edition

D. C. M. Yardley LLD (Birm), MA, D PHIL (Oxon)
of Gray's Inn, Barrister, Chairman of the Commission for Local Administration
in England; sometime Barber Professor of Law, University of Birmingham, and
Rank Foundation Professor of Law, University of Buckingham

London
Butterworths
1984

England	Butterworths & Co (Publishers) Ltd, 88 Kingsway, LONDON WC2B 6AB
Australia	Butterworth Pty Ltd, SYDNEY, MELBOURNE, BRISBANE, ADELAIDE and PERTH
Canada	Butterworth & Co (Canada) Ltd, TORONTO Butterworth & Co (Western Canada) Ltd, VANCOUVER
New Zealand	Butterworths of New Zealand Ltd, WELLINGTON
Singapore	Butterworth & Co (Asia) Pte Ltd, SINGAPORE
South Africa	Butterworth Publishers (Pty) Ltd, DURBAN
USA	Mason Publishing Co, ST PAUL, Minnesota Butterworth Legal Publishers, SEATTLE, Washington; BOSTON, Massachusetts; and AUSTIN, Texas D & S Publishers, CLEARWATER, Florida

© Butterworth & Co (Publishers) Ltd 1984

British Library Cataloguing in Publication Data

Yardley, D.C.M.
  Introduction to British constitutional law.—
  6th ed.
  1. Great Britain—Constitutional law
  I. Title
  344.102   KD 3989

  ISBN (Hardcover) 0-406-69007-3
  ISBN (Softcover) 0-406-69008-1

Typeset by Phoenix Photosetting, Chatham
Printed by Mackays of Chatham Ltd

To my wife

Preface to Sixth Edition

It is now nearly a quarter of a century since I completed writing the first edition of this book, and the pace of constitutional development in the intervening years has been distinctly lively. Although the essential plan and order of the book has remained intact through the whole of its life, much of the text has been altered to take account of the march of constitutional progress. On this occasion the major statutes which have caused revision include the Suppression of Terrorism Act 1978, the House of Commons (Redistribution of Seats) Act 1979, the Representation of the People Act 1981, the Supreme Court Act 1981, the British Nationality Act 1981, the Employment Act 1982, the Northern Ireland Act 1982, the Canada Act 1982 and the Representation of the People Act 1983. Provisions to rationalise and codify the law concerning police powers of search and arrest were included in the Police and Criminal Evidence Bill which was being considered by Parliament early in 1983. The Bill was controversial, and had already been amended in a number of respects before it lapsed when Parliament was dissolved in May. The intention to promote a similar measure in the new Parliament was announced in the Queen's Speech in June 1983, but it is too early to be able to forecast what form this will take. Accordingly I have for the present left untouched the passages in Chapter 8 which describe the current mix of common law and statute law on these subjects. It is also the declared intention of the government to bring forward legislation to abolish (and presumably redistribute the powers of) the Greater London Council, the Inner London Education Authority and the Metropolitan County Councils with effect from 1986. Again it is not possible in this edition to anticipate such proposed changes.

I have recorded the recent strengthening of the House of Commons Select Committee system. There is a short new passage on telephone tapping; and account is taken of several important court decisions in the areas of civil liberties, administrative law, and of the effect upon municipal law and parliamentary sovereignty of European Community regulations. The demise of the Scotland Act 1978 and the Wales Act 1978 has caused me to remove the tentative passages in the last edition concerned with devolution of some powers to Scotland and Wales; while the new passage on the Northern Ireland Act 1982 records the latest in a long line of efforts to find the germ of a constitutional solution for that unhappy province. Chapter 13 on the Commonwealth attempts to show the current position in a loose and ever-changing association. At the time of writing there are 48 full members of the Commonwealth, but it is still possible that others will join, some perhaps from outside the ranks of the remaining dependent territories. Thus the Republic of the Maldives, which had been a British protectorate from 1887 till it became independent in 1965, was admitted as a full member, with so-called 'special membership', in July 1982. Patriation of the Canadian Constitution by the Canada Act 1982 and recent developments in Australia have, however, enabled me to delete a section of the chapter which had explained the former anomalous duties of the United Kingdom Parliament in relation to constitutional matters in those countries.

Once again I have been fortunate in the comments and suggestions about the book which I have received from friends and colleagues, or in reviews, and I have tried to take account of them. Miss H. M. Webb of the Foreign and Commonwealth Office Library and Records Department was particularly generous in her efforts to assist me with up-to-date information on the Commonwealth. And the staff of Butterworths, as always, were understanding and helpful at all stages of the preparation of this edition.

Belbroughton Road, Oxford   D.C.M.Y.

November 1983

Extract from Preface to First Edition

The author of any new book on law should be able to justify its appearance, and that justification may be by no means apparent when the subject of the work has already occupied the attentions of writers before him. The leading textbooks upon the subject of constitutional law today are of such great merit that no teacher of the subject can do better than to recommend his pupils to be guided by them. It is perhaps invidious to identify these books here, but I have in mind particularly the comprehensive work of Professor Hood Phillips and also the slightly shorter volume of Professor Wade and Mr G. Godfrey Phillips. For further reading there are many books to be consulted—Ridges, Keir and Lawson, Dicey, Anson, Taswell Langmead, Griffith and Street, to mention but a few; and it would therefore seem that any new book in the field may be superfluous. Yet, because of the absence of any single document embodying the British Constitution, there are many students just embarking on their study of the subject who still find considerable difficulty in gaining a full picture of the area of law covered by it, and they are thus at somewhat of a disadvantage when reading the works I have already mentioned. In particular they find it hard to see how the constitutions of Commonwealth countries can have anything at all to do with the law of England, and also why the constitutional law of England, unlike other branches of English law, is usually applicable to the other parts of the United Kingdom. It is my hope that the present short work may do something to remedy this state of affairs. My intention is simply to draw a brief composite sketch of the field that any student of the subject must traverse, and to suggest the problems which exist rather than to attempt to solve them. Footnotes and authorities have been deliberately kept to the minimum. Historical material is only included where it is either still part of, or necessary for the understanding of, the modern law. At the end of each chapter, however, the reader will find a short list of recommended works which will enlighten the inquiring mind upon the details of the subject. Although it is hoped that the book is intelligible to laymen, I think that most readers will already have some acquaintance with the general principles of English law and the history of the judicial system.

This volume is therefore directed primarily towards the needs of university law students just beginning their study of constitutional law, and of students who are reading for professional examinations, such as Part I of the Bar examination. But it is also hoped that those students of other subjects who require a certain knowledge of the law of the Constitution will find the present account meets their needs.

I have been very fortunate in the encouragement and help received while preparing this book. Professor H. G. Hanbury, Fellow of All Souls College, Oxford, Professor O. Hood Phillips of the University of Birmingham and Mr G. H. Treitel, Fellow of Magdalen College, Oxford, have all read the draft typescript, and most of the improvements incorporated thereafter have been due to their thoughtful and constructive criticism. Even where I have been unable to accept such criticism its very existence has caused me to re-examine what I had previously written with the intention of making my point a little clearer. For any faults that remain I am, of course, solely responsible, and any views expressed upon the law are mine alone. I should also like to thank the publishers for their consideration and help at all stages of the writing of this work. But most of all my debt is to my pupils. It has often appeared to me that I learn far more from them than they do from me, and it is my hope that I have been able to repay some part of that debt in writing this book.

St Edmund Hall, Oxford   D.C.M.Y.

27 November 1959

Contents

Table of Statutes

List of Cases

Part 1

Principles of British Constitutional Law

Chapter 1

The Nature of British Constitutional Law

It is very difficult to define the term 'constitutional law' as applied to the United Kingdom of Great Britain and Northern Ireland. Naturally it must be that law which is concerned with the constitution of the country.[1] But, whereas in the great majority of the nations of the civilised world it is possible to discover a single document or bundle of documents which embody the constitution of the country concerned, in this country there is no such guide. The provisions of our constitution must be gleaned from among the vast mass of source-material which together forms the whole body of English, Scots and Northern Ireland law. This law is derived partly from custom, but mostly from written sources, namely reports of decided cases, statutes (which, as we shall see in Chapter 2, override any already existing legal rules which conflict with them) and occasionally the writings of jurists, though these latter are only called into account where other guidance for the courts is lacking. The scope of the law is practically unlimited, for it must cover all aspects of the relationships between the individuals and authorities throughout the country. Thus it is inevitable that there should be legal rules concerning crime, matrimonial relationships, real and personal property, conveyancing, wills, sale, civil wrongs, the status of companies, aeronautics and the control of health, to mention but a few topics. But it is necessary for the constitutional lawyer to divine what, out of the whole mass of the law of the United Kingdom, amounts to part of the constitution.

Professor Hood Phillips has defined the constitution of a

---

1 It is not intended to explore the meaning of the word 'law' in these pages. This has been the subject of much jurisprudential thought, for which the standard works on jurisprudence should be consulted. Suffice it to say here that law amounts to those rules which the courts of law are bound to enforce.

state as 'the system of laws, customs and conventions which define the composition and powers of organs of the state, and regulate the relations of the various state organs to one another and to the private citizen'.[2] It is submitted that the constitution of any country must comprise the fundamental structure and organisation of that country, and that therefore constitutional law is its fundamental law, its basic, essential law, whether it be civil, criminal, public or private, together with those rules of conduct laid down to govern the exercise of state power by the official organs of the state. If this postulate is accepted as of general application throughout the world, then it must be accepted for the United Kingdom. It is thus the task of any British lawyer concerned with the constitution to determine which laws out of the whole body of United Kingdom law come within the realm of constitutional law. Since there is no United Kingdom constitutional instrument boldly laying down the laws of the constitution, and showing the lawyer where the line is to be drawn, any assessment of what laws come within the field which is the subject of this book remains largely a matter of personal opinion. It is only rarely that a court of law expresses any opinion on the distinction, for provided the court is able to deduce the law applicable in a given case, it is not often concerned to declare which branch of United Kingdom law it may belong to in comparison with other branches. Sometimes the true classification of a legal rule must remain a matter of doubt, but on the other hand there are frequent occasions when the problem is by no means insoluble. For example, it is a rule of English law that any person who inflicts injury upon another by reason of negligence will be liable to pay damages to that other person, though these damages may be reduced if there has been contributory negligence on the part of the injured person. It would be quite possible in the future for Parliament to enact a statute to the effect that contributory negligence should cease to be a defence in an action for negligence, and the effect would be an alteration of one of the branches of the law of torts. But the *method* by which such change had come about (ie parliamentary legislation) would not have been altered at all.

It is not contended that this fundamental law of the state is unalterable. It is normal in most countries that the law of the

---

2   *Constitutional and Administrative Law* (6th edn, 1978) p 5.

constitution should provide within itself for the method of its own alteration. Often this is a method quite different from that employed when altering or repealing laws which do not form part of the constitution. To give but one example,[3] the constitutional document of the United States of America provides that any amendment of the constitution may be carried out either by (1) initiation of at least two-thirds of each House of Congress, and ratification by a majority in the legislature of at least three-quarters of the states, or by (2) initiation of a convention called on the application of the legislatures of at least two-thirds of the states, and ratification by conventions in at least three-quarters of the states, provided in either case that no state, without its own consent, may be deprived of its equal representation in the Senate.[4] These are perhaps fairly complicated methods of change, though only the first method has ever been used, and the position is quite different in this country, where constitutional change may be brought about in the same way as any other change of the law, namely by simple Act of the United Kingdom Parliament.

In many countries the constitution comes into being as the result of a political upheaval, as in the USA, where the constitution which came into force on 4 March 1789 was the political result of the War of Independence. In Eastern Europe after the Second World War the new political masters of most of the Russian satellite countries were able to overthrow the previously existing constitutions, and to impose their own will in fresh constitutions. At all events, whatever the executive regime of a particular nation, the constitution inevitably follows from the fact of national political independence. Any such independent country may enact its own laws, including its fundamental laws, for no machinery exists to stop it from doing so. A lawyer is not professionally concerned with politics, and must confine himself to the realms of pure law, but such law is always dependent upon political fact. Jurists have frequently studied the questions of how rules become law, how a constitution comes into being, and who has the power legally to conceive or enact a constitution. But these questions, with which we are not

---

3 Other instances may be seen in Chapter 13, below, in the other independent countries of the Commonwealth.

4 Constitution of the United States of America, art V.

concerned here, must, it is submitted, always remain theoretical, and have little relation to the reality of state necessity and state power. Nevertheless, once a constitution exists, the lawyer must seek to enforce it and to carry it out.

As has been stated above, United Kingdom constitutional law comprises all those laws, derived from the various sources referred to above, which are fundamental to the organisation of the state, together with such lesser rules as are laid down to facilitate the working of the organisation, but it also includes a certain element of pure convention. It must be admitted that there is here a contradiction in terms. Conventions are mentioned separately because they are not laws, and the courts are therefore not bound to enforce them. They certainly do not amount to law, but they are regarded as being of so fundamental a nature that it would be unthinkable that anyone should transgress them. Also, on the rare occasions when a constitutional convention has been flouted the result has sometimes been that the convention is made into binding law by Parliament.[5] Such conventions may come into being in various ways, but normally they are said to exist because of long usage or of agreement, and because everyone is entitled to expect that they always will be followed in suitable circumstances.

Because of their practical importance, it may be suggested that constitutional conventions form the very essence or basis of the British unwritten constitution. Instances of these conventions include the rule that the monarch will exercise his royal prerogative (with a few exceptions) only with the advice of his ministers, and that the ministers of the Crown are collectively responsible to Parliament for the acts of any one of their number in his capacity as a minister. Other important conventions will be mentioned in the appropriate sections of this book. But it may be as well here to note the most basic convention of all, that the government must not flout the generally expressed wishes of Parliament, and that it must not impede the lawful activities of the members of the Opposition. Thus it was that in 1979 the Prime Minister of the day, Mr James Callaghan, advised the Queen to dissolve Parliament so that a General Election could be held. This was after a motion of no confidence in Her

---

5   Eg as happened at the time of the passing of the Parliament Act 1911: Chapter 2, below.

Majesty's Government had been carried by a majority of one vote in a specially arranged debate in the House of Commons, the first time that such a vote had been carried in the Commons since 1924. It is because the necessary conventions have not had a chance to grow up gradually that a newly independent Commonwealth country's constitutional document, incorporating the *legal* part of the constitution but not its spirit, may sometimes fail, and even give rise to absolutism.

ENGLISH LAW AND BRITISH CONSTITUTIONAL LAW

The term 'British constitutional law' is used in the title of this present chapter. Yet, as all lawyers are brought up to remember, English law and Scots law are quite different bodies of rules, with distinct traditions and histories, even though in certain fields they have come to bear similarities to each other. Again, the law of Northern Ireland is separate from either of these two systems, and so is that of the Isle of Man and of the Channel Islands. Only between England and Wales has a fusion of laws taken place, although the true reason from which this result followed was the subjugation of the latter country by the former in the middle ages. England, Wales and Scotland together form Great Britain; and Great Britain together with Northern Ireland forms the United Kingdom: this latter body alone is recognised as the state for international purposes. The United Kingdom together with the Isle of Man and the Channel Islands form the British Isles.[6] Each of these countries, other than England and Wales, whose laws and institutions are the same, will be dealt with separately in Chapter 7 below, but for the present it is probably enough to say, in explanation of the phrase used in the chapter heading, that the constitutional laws of England and Scotland have become substantially identical, save in rare instances, and save for nomenclature,[7] and that Northern Ireland, though until 1972 it maintained its own local Parliament and executive, has always been part of the one Union

---

6 Strictly speaking the Republic of Ireland also falls geographically within the British Isles, but it is now a completely independent country and outside the Commonwealth.

7 Eg *MacCormick v Lord Advocate* 1953 SC396 (see Chapter 2, below); also the entirely different system of courts (Chapter 7, below.)

as far as international affairs are concerned,[8] and its laws are for the most part similar to those of England, the powers of any local legislature and executive being subject to those wielded at Westminster. The Channel Islands and the Isle of Man preserve the independence of their laws and institutions more or less intact. The term 'British constitutional law' is justified in that the principles to be stated in this book are mostly common to England, Wales and Scotland, and are often similar in Northern Ireland, while they have a particular effect upon the Isle of Man and the Channel Islands. It is this common constitutional law which is of significance when considering the home country as the centre of the Commonwealth.[9]

THE SUBJECTS COVERED BY BRITISH CONSTITUTIONAL LAW

Although, as has been pointed out above, the identity of the actual rules which come within the scope of our fundamental law may be the subject of dispute, it is submitted that the following short list probably covers the field:

1 the law concerning the composition of the national legislature and legislative powers;
2 the law concerning the composition and functions of central government;
3 the law concerning the composition and powers of any subordinate or devolved legislature or executive within the United Kingdom;
4 the hierarchy and status of courts of law;
5 the limits of personal liberty and the rights of the individual;
6 the relationship between the executive and the individual;
7 the law of citizenship and the status of aliens;
8 the status of certain national institutions, such as the armed forces and the Church;
9 the relations between central and local government; and
10 the relationship between the United Kingdom and its dependencies, and with the independent members of the Commonwealth.

It is on the basis of this list that the remainder of the book will be framed.

---

8   Thus, citizens of the United Kingdom all bear the same nationality and status; see Chapter 8, below.
9   See Chapter 13, below.

FURTHER READING

O. Hood Phillips *Constitutional and Administrative Law* (6th edn, 1978)

E. C. S. Wade and G. Godfrey Phillips *Constitutional and Administrative Law* (9th edn, by A. W. Bradley, 1977)

A. V. Dicey *Introduction to the Study of the Law of the Constitution* (10th edn, by E. C. S. Wade, 1959)

Sir W. Ivor Jennings *The Law and the Constitution* (5th edn, 1959)

Sir W. Ivor Jennings *The British Constitution* (5th edn, 1966)

Sir D. L. Keir and F. H. Lawson *Cases in Constitutional Law* (6th edn, by F. H. Lawson and D. J. Bentley, 1979)

G. Marshall and G. C. Moodie *Some Problems of the Constitution* (4th edn, 1967)

R. F. V. Heuston *Essays in Constitutional Law* (2nd edn, 1964)

J. D. B. Mitchell *Constitutional Law* (2nd edn, 1968)

Geoffrey Wilson *Cases and Materials on Constitutional and Administrative Law* (2nd edn, 1976)

O. Hood Phillips *Reform of the Constitution* (1970)

S. A. de Smith *Constitutional and Administrative Law* (4th edn, by H. Street and R. Brazier, 1981)

G. Marshall *Constitutional Theory* (1971)

Chapter 2

Parliament

Parliament is the primary legislative organ of the United Kingdom, and its most important function is to make laws. Obedience to these laws is obligatory upon all people who owe allegiance to the Crown and who are present within the United Kingdom.[1] In certain respects Parliament has refrained from exercising jurisdiction over the Channel Islands and the Isle of Man,[2] and also at times over Northern Ireland.[3] Parliament sits at Westminster, and has sometimes been known as the Imperial Parliament, as it also has the right to legislate for British dependencies and, within severe limits, for other parts of the Commonwealth.[4] Other important functions of Parliament include discussion of policy, and the surveillance of the government. It is necessary to consider six aspects of Parliament in this chapter, namely the composition of Parliament, the duration of Parliament, the procedure for making laws, other functions of Parliament, parliamentary privilege and the sovereignty of Parliament.

I. Composition of Parliament

There are three component parts of Parliament, the monarch, the House of Lords and the House of Commons. It is more usual to regard Parliament as composed of only the two Houses, which

---

1 Allegiance does not necessarily depend only upon the possession of British citizenship. The concept of British citizenship is now, in any case, fairly complicated, and will be explained shortly in Chapter 8, below. Again, allegiance does not depend only on residence, but it is sufficient in this chapter to say that allegiance may be either permanent or temporary: the whole problem will be discussed in Chapter 8.
2 See Chapter 7, below.
3 See Chapter 7, below.
4 This will be explained in Chapter 13, below.

sit at Westminster, but it is strictly correct to consider all three elements as part of the whole, for no legislation can come into being without the participation of the monarch, as will be seen presently. The institution of the monarchy itself will, however, be examined in Chapter 3 rather than in the present chapter.

THE HOUSE OF LORDS

The House of Lords is the successor of the old *Curia Regis*, which comprised the King's advisers, but the House itself, as a gathering of all the noblemen of the land, probably stems from sometime in the thirteenth century. One great difference between the modern House of Lords and the Curia is that the latter was a feudal body, whereas feudalism now plays no part in our law or society. The membership of the House has altered comparatively little since earliest times, though there have been several recent modifications. At present there are over 1000 people qualified to sit in the Lords, though many do not exercise their right to do so. Membership is comprised as follows:

A. *The Lords Temporal*, who may be subdivided into:

1 All hereditary peers and peeresses of the realm, except Irish peers. This group does not include heirs to peerages who merely hold courtesy titles and are not in fact the head of their line.[5] Peers in their own right include dukes not of royal blood, marquesses, earls, viscounts and barons, and they currently number about 750.[6] Under the Peerage Act 1963, however, it is now possible for any peer to disclaim his peerage for the duration of his life, leaving his next heir to decide whether or not he also will surrender the peerage when the time comes for him to succeed to the title. The main purpose of this new function is to enable those who wish to sit in the House of Commons, if duly elected, to escape the automatic disqualification (mentioned below) which attaches to a peer. Under a Standing Order of the House of Lords a procedure has also been established whereby peers who do not wish to attend the

5 Irish peers, and all persons who possess courtesy titles, rather than peerages, are eligible to sit in the House of Commons, if elected: see below.
6 In November 1981 there were 769, but the number is gradually reduced by extinction of title whenever a peer dies without an heir.

House regularly may obtain, or even sometimes be assumed to have obtained, leave of absence. Although this cannot legally prevent a peer from sitting whenever he so desires, it does nevertheless have this practical effect, thus discouraging the occasional attendance in the legislature of noble 'backwoodsmen'.

2 All life peers created by the monarch, under the terms of the Life Peerages Act 1958. Any man or woman may receive the rank of baron under this Act, which was passed as a step towards reform of the composition of the House. Objection may be raised that in fact the government of the day may nominate its own supporters as life peers, but it seems that at present none of the major political parties are likely to abuse the power conferred by the Act, which has been used partly to boost the Labour benches in the Lords, and partly to give seats in the chamber to people eminent in divers walks of life. In November 1981 there were 330 life peers.

3 The eleven Lords of Appeal in Ordinary ('Law Lords'), who are life peers appointed under the terms of the Appellate Jurisdiction Act 1876, as subsequently amended.[7]

B. The Lords Spiritual, who are the Archbishops of Canterbury and York, the Bishops of London, Durham and Winchester, and the 21 most senior other diocesan bishops of the Church of England, according to seniority of appointment. The Bishop of Sodor and Man, however, never has a seat in the House, as he is always a member of the Tynwald of the Isle of Man.[8]

There are, however, certain disqualifications which will prevent a peer from being able to take his seat in the House, although he would otherwise have been entitled to do so. These disqualifications apply to:

1 aliens;
2 peers under the age of 21;
3 persons convicted of treason;
4 members expelled by the House acting as a court of law,[9] unless pardoned; and
5 bankrupts.

---

7 The Act of 1876 originally provided for the appointment of only two Lords of Appeal in Ordinary.
8 See Chapter 7, below.
9 A peer expelled by a resolution of the House of Lords acting as a legislative body cannot be excluded permanently. The judicial functions of the House will be discussed later in Chapter 4.

The Speaker of the House of Lords is the Lord Chancellor, who is also a member of the government, and is not therefore expected to be impartial in party matters.[10] The political parties maintain supporters in the House, each party having its Leader, but since the peers do not become members of the House by election as party candidates there are many peers who have no political affiliations at all. The Conservative Party has often been able to rally sufficient support to ensure a majority in any critical debate or measure, though this power has been affected by the modern practice of appointing life peers, as shown above. But in any case, as we shall see when examining the functions of Parliament, party politics play a much smaller role in the Lords than in the House of Commons. In the Queen's Speech at the opening of Parliament in 1967, the Labour Government stated its intention to initiate legislation to reform the House of Lords still further, and this intention was reaffirmed in 1968, but the Parliament (No 2) Bill, which was designed to achieve such a reform, had to be abandoned in 1969 because of determined opposition from a number of back benchers on both sides of the House of Commons.

The Labour Party Conference in 1977 voted overwhelmingly for total abolition of the House of Lords. On the other hand a review committee set up by the Conservative Party reported in 1978 in favour of retention of the House with a reformed composition, consisting of two-thirds elected and one-third nominated members. Many other schemes for reform of the composition of the House of Lords, and sometimes of its powers, have been put forward from time to time; and there is a general recognition that the present composition is very difficult to defend in a modern democratic state, however well the house may do its work in practice. It seems realistic to expect eventual reform, though not abolition, of the second chamber.

THE HOUSE OF COMMONS

The House of Commons, sometimes known as the lower House of Parliament, is a representative assembly. Its history dates from the thirteenth century, and the methods of providing

---

10 The Lord Chancellor need not strictly be a peer, but according to modern practice he always is, even if this involves the special conferment of a peerage upon him on appointment to his office.

representatives to sit in the House have altered very greatly in the course of its existence, particularly as a result of the Reform Acts of the nineteenth century. Today there are 650 members of Parliament (MPs), and each is elected by universal adult suffrage in one of the parliamentary constituencies in the United Kingdom. The total number of MPs was recently increased, partly because of an increase in the representation at Westminster from Northern Ireland (effected by the House of Commons (Redistribution of Seats) Act 1979), and partly as a result of a redistribution of the seats currently for Great Britain. The whole of the Kingdom is divided into these constituencies according to roughly equal groups of population. There is no limit to the number of candidates who may offer themselves for election in each constituency, though each must deposit £150 with the returning officer of the constituency, and this sum will be forfeited by the candidate if he fails to poll at least one-eighth of the total votes cast. The great majority of candidates belong to political parties, the most powerful of which are the Conservative, Labour, Liberal, Social Democratic, Official Unionist, and Scottish and Welsh National Parties, and successful candidates will support or oppose the government party according to their affiliation. But in law a candidate's or member's affiliation to a party is ignored: his status as a member of Parliament alone, if he is elected, is all that is recognised.[11]

Anyone may 'stand for Parliament',[12] but the following persons are disqualified from sitting in the House:

1 aliens;
2 persons under the age of 21;
3 those convicted of treason or serving a term of imprisonment or detention for more than one year; (If an MP is sentenced for any other offence to a period of imprisonment the Speaker must be informed, but the member is not expelled from the House unless a motion to expel him has been passed.)
4 certain persons suffering from mental illness;

11 The existence of political parties is, however, apparently assumed by the terms of the Ministers of the Crown Act 1937, and the post of Leader of the Opposition is recognised in that statute.
12 Under the Representation of the People Act 1981 those disqualified from election to the Commons because they are serving a term of imprisonment or detention for more than one year are also disqualified from being nominated for election.

5 peers and peeresses in their own right, other than the holders of Irish peerages;
6 clergy of the Church of England and the Church of Ireland, ministers of the Church of Scotland, and priests of the Roman Catholic Church. Although none of these churches is represented directly in the Commons, the Church of England is represented, as has been seen, by its bishops in the Lords. Clergy of the Church in Wales may, however, sit in the Commons as a result of the Welsh Church Act 1914;
7 bankrupts;
8 anyone guilty of corrupt or illegal practices at parliamentary elections. These terms are statutorily defined, and the consequences of disqualification are dealt with in the House of Commons Disqualification Act 1975;
9 judges of the Supreme Court of Judicature and the Crown and County Courts, and stipendiary magistrates;
10 civil servants, police officers and members of the armed forces on the active list;
11 sheriffs, and returning officers as regards the constituencies of which they are returning officers;
12 members of non-Commonwealth legislatures; and
13 holders of certain specified offices, listed in section 1 and the First Schedule of the House of Commons Disqualification Act 1975.[13] These are usually offices of profit, but the Act also preserves the traditional method whereby an MP may resign from the House, namely by applying for one of the sinecure positions of Steward of the Chiltern Hundreds or of the Manor of Northstead.

The chairman of the House is the Speaker, who is elected from among its members by the whole House at the beginning of each Parliament. The election is often unanimous after the Government party and the Opposition have held informal discussions upon the subject.[14] The political division of the members is far more pronounced than in the House of Lords. The government, headed by the Prime Minister, is normally formed from the party which has the largest group of members in the Commons, and which then becomes known as the government party. The

13 The House of Commons Disqualification Act 1975 also lays down that no more than 95 members may hold ministerial office.
14 The election was contested in 1951 and 1970.

Prime Minister will appoint an influential member of this party as Leader of the House. Members of parties which oppose the government party are then termed the Opposition, and the most powerful Opposition party will elect one of its number to be Leader of the Opposition. The support of members of either the government or Opposition parties in any vote is ensured by means of the 'Whips', who are MPs chosen within the party concerned, or by the Prime Minister for the government party, to maintain party discipline and regularity of attendance at the House on important occasions. Although 'Whips' also function in the House of Lords their importance is not so great there, partly because of the large number of independent members in that House, and partly because, as we shall see presently, the Lords have far less power than the House of Commons. Government 'Whips' hold titular posts as Lords of the Treasury or members of the Royal Household. The strict party system in the Commons may in some measure detract from the quality of debate in that chamber, and it does tend to prevent members from voting according to conscience; but on the other hand the stability, both within the House and of the government – for, as we shall see in the next chapter, the existence of the government depends on the continued support of the majority in the Commons – contributes greatly to the general stability of the country, and enables the House to work through a lot of business without undue hindrance.

II. Duration of Parliament

Section 7 of the Parliament Act 1911 enacts that no Parliament may last for more than five years, and unless Parliament has already been dissolved by the monarch its life will terminate by lapse of time exactly five years after it came into being. A General Election of members of the Commons will then be held, although the composition of the Lords will not be altered by this event. It is, however, always open to Parliament to extend its own life by means of an Act of Parliament, and this has been done, for example, during the war of 1939–1945; but it is conventional to effect this prolongation only from year to year. Casual vacancies in the Commons are filled by holding a by-election in any constituency affected.

Each new Parliament is summoned by the monarch, and

divides its time into sessions, normally covering periods of about one year each, though they are sometimes held more frequently. Sessions are ended by the monarch 'proroguing' Parliament. The sittings of Parliament within each session are also divided up by periods of 'recess'.

III. Procedure for Making Laws

A law is made by the passing of a statute through Parliament. In the course of its passage it is known as a Bill, but when it is passed it becomes an Act of Parliament. Such Acts must be approved by a majority of the votes cast in each House, and then receive the assent of the monarch. Certain exceptions to this procedure of the passage of a Bill through both Houses are provided for in the Parliament Acts 1911 and 1949, which will be discussed later in this chapter. There are three main kinds of Bill, Public, Private and Hybrid. Public Bills concern law which will be of general application when it is passed. Private Bills are measures dealing with personal matters or local matters in a certain area of the country only. Hybrid Bills are otherwise Public Bills which nevertheless affect private interests in such a way as to render it desirable that part of the procedure for Private Bills be adapted for their passage. The procedure for the passage of each of these types of measure will be sketched in these pages, but first it should be noted that such procedure is conventional only, save where the Parliament Acts 1911 and 1949 apply. It is within the competence of either House to vary its procedure, yet the conventional practice is unlikely to be disturbed. Bills will be either Government Bills (that is, introduced by a member of either House who is also a minister) or Private Members' Bills (introduced by a member of the House who is not a member of the government, or who is introducing the Bill purely in his private capacity as a member of the House). Government Bills occupy far more time in Parliament, because parliamentary time is allocated by the Leader of the House, and very little time is allotted to Private Members' Bills. In fact only certain Fridays of the year are currently set aside for this purpose, and members wishing to introduce such Bills must ballot for the right to do so on one of these days. It may be thought that in practice too little time is now allowed for the consideration of Private Members' Bills, which are often of greater importance than the time spent on them would suggest. They do indeed provide the ordinary citizen with the opportunity to initiate legislation which is not necessarily of importance to the government. Such measures were the far-reaching Matrimonial Causes Act 1937, introduced by Mr (later Sir) A. P. Herbert, and the Murder (Abolition of Death Penalty) Act 1965, introduced by Mr Silverman.

A. PUBLIC BILLS

These Bills may originate in either House, although most Bills in fact go through the Commons before the Lords, and Money Bills and other Bills with financial clauses may not originate in the House of Lords, but the procedure is largely similar in both Houses. The member introducing the Bill will either present it at the Table of the House or, more rarely, move for leave to introduce it.[15] In either case the member will previously have given notice of his intention. There then follow at intervals the first and second readings, the committee stage, the report stage and the third reading. The first reading is purely formal, when the Clerk of the House reads out the title of the Bill only. The second reading, however, is the vital stage at which it is decided whether a Bill will be defeated out of hand or will go forward for further consideration. Normally the member who introduced the Bill will speak in its favour, pointing out the main principles involved. There is no possibility of altering details at this stage, and the Bill must stand or fall on its general merits. If the Bill is unopposed, then it will be 'read' a second time very quickly, but if it is opposed then a debate on the principles of the Bill will take place, after which a vote is taken. Of course a Government Bill is very unlikely to be defeated, but a Private Member's Bill is by no means as certain to be approved at this stage, as voting is rarely on party lines. In 1965 an alternative procedure for the second reading of Public Bills in the Commons was introduced, whereby a minister may move that any such Bill be referred to a standing Second Reading Committee, consisting of from 30 to 80 MPs,

---

15 Private members also have the privilege of moving for leave to introduce Bills after 'Government business' on any day, but as only ten minutes are allowed for each such introduction, plus ten minutes for any opposition, little more than publicity is likely to result.

which shall then report to the House, with reasons, whether or not they recommend that the Bill be read a second time. The procedure may not be used if at least 20 members rise in their places to object to the minister's motion. But if a Bill is sent to the Second Reading Committee, the report of the Committee must be put to the House for a vote without amendment or debate. This has resulted in a saving of parliamentary time, and the passage of many non-controversial Bills for which the government would not otherwise have been able to find debating time. Since 1979 all Private Members' Bills have automatically been referred to the Second Reading Committee. Another reform introduced at the same time, and also aimed at time-saving, was the limitation of speeches in Second Reading debates in the Commons to ten minutes.

If the Bill is defeated at its second reading it is then withdrawn, but if it is approved by a majority of the voters in the count it goes on into the committee stage. In this stage a committee of the House, whose membership is allotted in the proportion that the parties have in the House, or in some cases a committee consisting of the whole House, will consider the detailed provisions or clauses, as they are called, of the Bill. In the consideration of a very long Bill time limits sometimes have to be set for this stage,[16] but usually the committee is able to discuss and alter if necessary any part of the Bill it thinks fit. At this stage the party majority of the government is not so important, as voting is not upon the general principles of the Bill, now accepted, but merely upon how best to formulate the detailed provisions throughout the Bill. In 1980 the Commons began the experiment of sending certain Bills for their committee stage to a Special Standing Committee. The main advantage of this has been that such a committee has been given the power to hold sittings at which evidence may be taken from outsiders, thus going some way towards the committee stage practice for Private Bills, mentioned below. After the committee stage is over the committee reports to the whole House what it has done. At this, the report stage, it is still possible for the House to

---

16 The 'Kangaroo' (only certain amendments are chosen for debate); the 'Guillotine' (a time limit is placed on the debate of each part of a measure); and the 'Closure' (an overall time-limit is placed on consideration of the Bill). These methods are not confined, however, to debate in committee.

amend the Bill, but this is not often done in practice. Finally the Bill receives its third reading, when a last debate is held upon the general principles of the measure. Again it is possible for the Bill to be defeated, but if it has already passed the other stages, particularly the second reading, it is most unlikely that this will occur. As far as details are concerned it is usual that only amendments of slips in the wording of the Bill are made. Once it has passed the third reading it has 'passed the House'. In 1967 the House of Commons' Select Committee on Procedure made recommendations designed to cut out waste of time and repetition of debate in the report stage and third reading of Public Bills, and as a result these last stages have for many Bills now been largely combined in practice.

Having been approved in one House, the Bill must now go to the other House and pass through similar stages in the course of the same session of Parliament. If the Bill should be approved in the second House in the same form in which it eventually passed the first House, then it will be sent forthwith for the Royal Assent, and will become an Act of Parliament. If on the other hand it is approved in principle, but altered in some respect in its details, then it will be returned for further consideration in the first House. If the amendments of the second chamber are then agreed to in the first chamber the Bill will go for the Royal Assent, but if no such agreement can be reached after a reasonable time the Bill was, up till 1911, treated as defeated, just as if the second House had rejected the Bill outright. The Parliament Acts of 1911 and 1949 have, however, altered this position greatly, and the effect of these Acts will be considered after the procedure for other types of Bill has been discussed.

B. PRIVATE BILLS

Private Bills are either local or personal. Local Private Bills for the most part concern some particular locality in the country, and are usually initiated by local authorities, whereas personal Private Bills deal with the affairs of certain particular persons or estates. Not all personal Bills, however, are necessarily Private Bills, and, for example, personal Indemnity Bills are usually Public Bills. Local Bills may be considered first in either House, but personal Private Bills must go through the Lords before the Commons. In each House the stages of the Bill are for the most part similar to those employed in the case of Public Bills, but a major difference appears in committee, for at that stage any interested party at all may appear and oppose the Bill, and witnesses may be called, so that the procedure takes on a quasi-judicial aspect. In addition the members of the committee who conduct this inquiry must be entirely disinterested in the affairs concerned in the Bill. This procedure is the outcome of a desire to protect the interests of those affected parties whose causes would not be likely to excite public interest. Once a Private Bill has passed one House it is unlikely to be altered or opposed in the other, though this does occasionally occur. After passing both Houses, the Bill goes for the Royal Assent.

C. HYBRID BILLS

When a Hybrid Bill is under consideration the opportunity for interested parties to appear at the committee stage must be given, but otherwise the procedure adopted is similar to that where a Public Bill is under consideration. Thus the members of the committee need not be disinterested.

In the case of all Bills the Royal Assent is required before they become law. Sometimes a Norman-French formula is used to signify the assent, though it is not customary now for the monarch to assent in person. But the assent is usually just notified to each House by the Speaker of the Commons and the Lord Chancellor respectively, under the powers provided in the Royal Assent Act 1967.

The Parliament Acts 1911 and 1949

From the foregoing account it will be seen that originally it was possible for either House to veto the legislative endeavours of the other by refusing to pass Bills sent to it from the other. Convention had it that the non-representative chamber, the Lords, should not so obstruct the Commons if the Commons had become set upon the passage of a particular measure, but nevertheless the Lords broke this convention several times during 1908 and 1909, when the Commons had a huge Liberal Party majority. After two general elections and considerable political rancour and bitterness, the government prevailed upon the Lords to allow a Parliament Bill to pass the upper chamber, by holding over it the promise of the King that he would if necessary create a sufficient number of new peers who would support its passage. The provisions of the resulting Parliament Act 1911 were altered even further to the detriment of the power of the Lords by the Parliament Act 1949, which was passed under the procedure laid down in the Act of 1911. The procedure provided for in the two Acts is as follows:

1   In the case of a *Money Bill* having passed the Commons, it shall receive the Royal Assent without the approval of the Lords unless it has been passed by the Lords within one month of being sent to the Lords, provided that the Bill was sent to the Lords at least one month before the end of the session. This, therefore, strengthens the previous constitutional convention that financial Bills should only begin in the Commons, and should not be altered by the Lords. The Acts provide guidance for the Speaker of the Commons as to what Bills are properly to be regarded as Money Bills, but the Speaker is nevertheless legally empowered to certify any Bill as a Money Bill in theory, for the Acts provide that the Speaker's certificate to this effect is final and cannot be questioned in any court of law.

2   The power of the Lords to reject any Bill attempting to extend the maximum duration of Parliament beyond five years is left unimpaired.

3   In the case of any other *Public Bill* the power of the Lords to obstruct the wishes of the Commons by rejection, complete or partial, has been severely curtailed. Under the provisions of the Acts, if a Bill has been passed in the Commons and then rejected in the Lords, and in the next session of Parliament it is again passed by the Commons, but the House of Lords does not also pass it without amendments (except amendments approved by the Commons), then the Commons is empowered to send it up for the Royal Assent despite the Lords' opposition. It is also provided that at least one year must have elapsed between the second reading of the Bill in the Commons in the first session and the third reading in the Commons in the second session. When this procedure has been adopted because of the Lords' opposition to a Public Bill, the Speaker of the House of Commons must endorse the Bill

with a certificate that it has been passed by the Commons according to the procedure laid down in the Parliament Acts before it is sent up for the Royal Assent. Again this certificate is final.

It will be noted that the Acts do not deal with Private Bills, and therefore the power of the Lords to veto Private Bills if the House should so wish is left untouched. The Lords no longer has any practical power over Money Bills at all, and theoretically it would be possible for the Speaker to certify any Bill as a Money Bill, though an abuse of this authority would very probably have disastrous political repercussions. It is in any case most unlikely in the British parliamentary system that the Prime Minister would be able to persuade the Speaker to take such a step. The delaying power of the Lords over other Public Bills, with the one exception of Bills to extend the life of Parliament, is now just one year. Under the Act of 1911 it was two years, and this cutting down of the time was the raison d'être of the 1949 Act. The Parliament Acts make clear the Commons' control over public finances, and they assert the supremacy of the Commons over the Lords, though of course it would always be open to any Parliament to alter the position by future legislation. This is, however, most unlikely to occur so long as the Lords remains basically an hereditary chamber. One of the reasons why the parties have found it so difficult to formulate an agreement on the basis of which to reform the composition of the Lords has been that such agreed reform might have to carry with it an increase in the actual power of the second chamber. This largely explains the general opposition of the Labour Party to most schemes so far suggested. Although there is at present a permanent Conservative majority in the Lords, the Labour Party has often been reasonably content with this state of affairs because it is a largely powerless majority in any case of real conflict. The Parliament (No 2) Bill had to be abandoned in 1969 partly because so many MPs could see the impracticability of the clauses in it designed to reduce still further the Lords' power to delay legislation. Yet any reformed and reinvigorated House might be less helpless against the wishes of a resolute Commons. But there have been a few clashes between the government and the Lords in the past 20 years, and it is thought likely that some further effort to reform the House of Lords may be made in the near future.

It is, however, fair to add that the House of Lords has rarely intended to be obstructive during the past 75 years, and that the Lords' amendments to Bills are more often accepted by the Commons than rejected. The peers only rarely vote on strict party lines, and it may be asserted that the passage of the Parliament Acts in a sense proved to be the saviour of the upper House. Once it is clear that their will cannot prevail over the Commons, the efforts of peers in the discharge of their parliamentary functions have naturally become more consistently constructive. It is suggested that the House of Lords now exercises much more usefully than in former times those functions which the members of the famous Conference of 1917–1918, presided over by Lord Bryce, considered ought to be discharged by the second chamber. These functions are the examination and revision of Bills first dealt with in the Commons, the delaying of Bills for so long, and no longer, as may be needed to enable national opinion to be expressed upon them, the initiation of less controversial Bills which can be expected to pass through the Commons fairly easily, and the full and free discussion of important matters for which the Commons may not immediately be able to find time. A recent authority has asserted that the House of Lords is the best second chamber in the Commonwealth, and one which stands comparison with its counterparts in almost any developed country.[17]

IV. Other Functions of Parliament

It would be a great mistake to think of Parliament only as a legislative assembly. In fact legislative business occupies only about one-half of the time taken by the sittings of Parliament. Nevertheless it is the legislative business and power of Parliament which is of importance to lawyers, who are only concerned to discover and to apply law; and it is only when legislating that Parliament is responsible for the creation of law, as the term legislation itself would imply. It is therefore not necessary to elaborate here upon the other functions of Parliament, but, in order to aid a full understanding of Parliament, which is a

---

17 S. A. de Smith *Constitutional and Administrative Law* (4th edn, 1981) p 300.

deliberative as well as a legislative assembly, the most important of them at the present day will be listed:

1 General debate, which may take place in either House upon any subject it deems fit to examine. There is no necessity for there to be any vote upon a motion, but often such a vote does take place, and frequently along party lines. Some of the subjects chosen for debate are put forward by the government, and others by the Opposition, for the time of Parliament is allotted by the Leaders of each House partly to matters the government wishes discussed and partly to subjects chosen by the Opposition. Here, as in the second and third functions mentioned below, it can be seen that Parliament, or at least the House of Commons, acts as a bridge between the people and the government, through the agency of the people's elected representatives.

2 Questions may be addressed by any member, usually to a minister, upon any subject connected with the administration or public affairs for which the minister or member is officially responsible, providing that it does not concern proceedings pending in Parliament. Often the questions are suggested by constituents. It is obvious that unless a proper answer of a more or less satisfactory nature is made the subject is likely to give rise to some agitation. It may be noted here that one of the salient differences between the procedure of the United Kingdom Parliament and that of the United States Congress is that there is no 'question time' in the latter, largely because members of the government do not sit in Congress.

3 The making of ministerial statements, which may or may not be followed by debate.

4 Work in committees. This is often upon Bills, as has been seen above, but it may be upon matters of any kind referred for inquiry to a committee by the House. The Public Accounts Committee and the Select Committees on Estimates and on the Nationalised Industries for many years played an important part in keeping a check on the administrative process. In recent years Parliament has experimented with the introduction of other committees to investigate broad fields of administrative activity, and in 1979 the House of Commons reorganised its committee structure in order to gain much more control over the main functions of government. There

are now fourteen select committees (and four sub-committees) of the House, each charged with one of the main areas of government, such as defence, foreign affairs, home affairs, the Treasury and the Civil Service, etc. The committees are small, ranging in numbers from eight to eleven, and there is a fifteenth 'liaison' committee, consisting of the chairmen of these committees, which resolves all demarcation disputes between the committees. The general opinion is that the powers of these committees to interview and question ministers, who are normally prepared to attend on request, and then to report upon their findings have had a salutary effect in shifting some of the control of the executive arm of government back to the elected representatives of the people in the Commons. Occasionally joint committees of the two Houses sit for the purpose of discussing matters of common concern, and in particular there is a joint committee to consider all Bills covering statute law revision and the consolidation of previous enactments.

5 The consideration of the privileges of the two Houses, which will be discussed more fully below.

6 The House of Lords, but not the Commons, is also the highest court of appeal for England, Northern Ireland and, in civil cases only, for Scotland. This topic will be discussed in Chapter 4.

V. Parliamentary Privilege

In order that members of both Houses may carry out their tasks without undue interference or fear, certain privileges have attached to them since very early times. The historical reason for their existence is that Parliament is strictly the 'High Court of Parliament', and superior courts of law maintain similar privileges which protect them in the exercise of their judicial functions. Although they are mainly similar in each House, for the privileges belong essentially to Parliament as a whole, there are some differences in effect. The privileges common to members of both Houses are:

1 Freedom of speech in debate from any outside interference at all. This privilege has been undoubted since the ultimate

triumph of Parliament over Stuart despotism in the seventeenth century. The meaning of 'debate' appears to have been widened considerably, for this privilege covers also communications between members or made to members by their constituents upon parliamentary business. Such missives would therefore be immune from any operation of the law of libel, as they are considered by the House to be 'proceedings in Parliament'. A recent limitation upon the meaning of this phrase and upon this privilege which has been imposed by the House of Commons itself will be discussed below.

2 Freedom from arrest during sessions of Parliament and for 40 days before or after a session. A peer, however, remains permanently covered by this privilege. But it is not as wide as it may seem, for it probably only covers civil arrest, now practically unknown. It is still debatable whether a member of either House is privileged from arrest for summary offences, though the absence of authority upon the point shows its comparative practical unimportance. A Select Committee on Parliamentary Privilege recommended, in 1967, the abolition by statute of freedom from arrest so far as members of the House of Commons are concerned, though it has not yet been implemented.

3 The Commons have the right of access to the monarch through the Speaker, whereas each peer has theoretically the right of individual access, probably very rarely exercised.

4 Each House has the right to regulate the qualifications for its membership, subject to any statute which may have been passed on the subject, and to regulate its own internal proceedings. Thus, much of the foregoing account of procedure in the passing of Bills is a matter upon which the courts cannot inquire.

5 The right to impeach, that is, to try any person for any offence in the House of Lords, with the Commons acting as prosecutors. This appears now to be obsolete, not having been exercised for over 175 years, and its abolition was in any case recommended by the select committee in 1967. But impeachment is still a live possibility in the United States, where article II, s 4 of the constitution provides: 'The President, Vice-President and all Civil Officers of the United States shall be removed from Office on Impeachment for, and Conviction of, Treason, Bribery, or other High Crimes and

Misdemeanors'. In 1974 President Nixon became the first US President to resign office when the House of Representatives Judiciary Committee voted overwhelmingly to recommend to the House that he be impeached.

6 The right of each House to punish for breach of privilege or contempt of the House. The privileges are those listed in this chapter, but contempt may in theory be anything which offends the dignity of the House. Whether anything amounts to a contempt or a breach of privilege is for the House itself to decide, and the courts have no cognisance of such a problem, except in the one instance where either House punishes a person, as for example by imprisonment, for a breach of privilege, but gives a patently bad reason for doing so. On a subsequent application for habeas corpus[18] the court may declare the proceeding to be unlawful,[19] but if no reason for the claim of the House should be given it would be impossible for any court to interfere.[20] Punishment awarded by the House

---

18 See Chapter 8, below.

19 See eg *Stockdale v Hansard* (1839) 9 Ad & El 1. There a report of prison commissioners contained a libel of Stockdale, and the Commons had ordered the parliamentary printers, Messrs Hansard, to publish the report for sale to the public. In the subsequent libel action by Stockdale, Hansard, under instructions from the Commons, pleaded that the report had been published by order of the House, and that it was therefore covered by parliamentary privilege. The court held that this was not one of the privileges of the House. Freedom of speech covered papers passed between members themselves, but not those allowed to pass into the hands of the general public.

20 As occurred in the *Middlesex Sheriff's case* (1840) 11 Ad & El 273, which was the sequel to *Stockdale v Hansard*, above. The Commons had passed a resolution that the publication of reports etc was essential for the proper functioning of Parliament, and that the House had the sole right of judging the validity and extent of any privileges claimed. The House allowed the damages to be paid in Stockdale's case, but made it clear that any future attempt to bring such an action would itself amount to a contempt of the House. Nevertheless Stockdale proceeded to bring another similar action against Hansard, and judgment was given in Stockdale's favour in the absence of any plea by the defendant, but when the Sheriff of Middlesex levied the damages awarded in this latter case, and he refused to give the sum back when so ordered by the Commons, he was forthwith imprisoned by order of the Commons for contempt and breach of privilege of the House. Although the Sheriff applied for habeas corpus, his application failed because the Speaker's warrant of committal did not contain any reason for the allegation of contempt or breach of privilege.

Ultimately the Parliamentary Papers Act was passed in 1840 to make law the very extension of privilege which the Commons had claimed, and the Sheriff was set free when the session of Parliament ended shortly afterwards. The enactment of the statute may perhaps be regarded as an act of conscience by the Commons.

may be by imprisonment, fine (at present this is only possible in the Lords), reprimand, admonition or, in the case of a member of the House, expulsion. Legislation is expected shortly to give the Commons power to impose fines, but also to abolish the power of either House to imprison. The most common recent instances of the privilege to punish being exercised are concerned with contempt by journalists, and with disorderly behaviour in the House.

In addition to the above each House has certain other privileges. The Commons maintains the right to control finance and initiate financial legislation. Originally this was mere convention, but the existence of the privilege has been strengthened by statute in the Parliament Acts 1911 and 1949, as described above. The Commons also claims as a privilege that the Crown will place the best construction on its deliberations, a privilege now of no practical importance. The additional privileges of the Lords are more numerous, but of very little real importance. They include the right to summon judges for advice on questions of law (in practice now never exercised, because of the presence in the House of the Lords of Appeal in Ordinary since the Appellate Jurisdiction Act 1876),[21] exemption from jury service, and the right of any peer alone to enter a protest against any measure of the House in its Journals.

A final word on the subject of parliamentary privilege as a living issue should be said. The original reason for the existence of the privileges, that is to protect the *High Court* of Parliament, has practically disappeared, for, except where the House of Lords acts as a final court of appeal, the real functions of Parliament are now those of debate and legislation. It cannot any longer be the case that all the existing privileges are necessary to protect members in the discharge of their duties. In particular it may be argued that the power to punish should be transferred from the Houses themselves to the courts of law, so that the Houses may no longer seem to be judges in their own cause. Indeed it is possible that only the safeguarding of freedom of speech actually inside Parliament is now necessary to ensure the existence of a free and virile assembly. In the present state of

---

21 The judges were last summoned in an English appeal in *Allen v Flood* [1898] AC 1, and in a Scottish appeal in *Free Church of Scotland (General Assembly) v Lord Overtoun* [1904] AC 515.

the law, however, it is to be expected that members will not claim privilege frivolously or unless there is real need to do so. The record of the House of Lords in this respect has in modern times been good, and it is extremely rare today for any peer to claim privilege. On the other hand the Commons has in the present century acquired a certain notoriety for its eagerness to claim and assert privilege. A standing committee of the House, the Committee of Privileges, meets whenever needed to consider alleged cases referred to it and to advise the whole House upon its proper course of action. Divers activities of individuals outside the House may be held by the House to amount to contempt,[1] and the courts of law are powerless to decide otherwise.[2] Often the cases alleged are not really infringements of the necessary freedom of the House, but merely instances where MPs have felt annoyed about things said of them.[3] Public feeling has on occasions been roused by what one may well consider abuse of the essential privileges of the House. It is a subject which has been much canvassed in letters to newspapers – the writers themselves having been in danger of the wrath of the Commons! But the general public and the courts can work no changes or diminution in the power of the House. It is therefore for the House itself to use these powers with discretion and good sense; the virtue of the preservation of freedom should not be permitted to turn into the vice of tyranny. It was encouraging that on 8 July 1958,[4] the House decided by a small majority that a letter written by a member to a minister was not necessarily a 'proceeding in Parliament', thus rendering the writer immune from the law of defamation. Mr George Strauss MP had written a letter to the Paymaster-General, who represented the Minister of Power (a peer) in the Commons. In it he alleged that the London Electricity Board had behaved in a scandalous manner in the way in which it invited tenders for the purchase of its scrap metal. The contents of the letter were disclosed to the Board, which, after some exchange of

1 Eg *R v Paty* (1704) 2 Ld Raym 1105, where five Aylesbury men had brought an action against the returning officers for refusing their votes at an election. They were committed to prison by order of the Commons for breach of privilege.
2 Eg *Middlesex Sheriff's case* (see note 20, p 28, above).
3 Eg the offence taken by MPs at the comments in the *Sunday Express* upon the methods of allocating petrol ration coupons: 563 HCDeb407 (1957).
4 591 HC Deb 208.

correspondence, informed Mr Strauss that it intended to sue him for libel. Although Mr Strauss claimed that this was a breach of the privileges of the House, a claim which was supported by the Report to the House of the Committee of Privileges, this claim was rejected on a free vote in the House. The status of such letters in the future will depend upon their actual nature, and their writers will only be absolutely privileged where the contents can be truly considered to pertain to parliamentary business, or the duty of the writer as a member of one of the Houses of Parliament.

It is perhaps worth noting that, as a result of a subsequent official inquiry into the activities of the London Electricity Board, it was found that no such irregularities as had been alleged in Mr Strauss's letter had in fact taken place. The present indications are that MPs since the Strauss affair have been more circumspect about claiming that their privileges have been infringed,[5] and in 1967 the Select Committee on Parliamentary Privilege set up by the Commons recommended a number of changes in procedure to reduce the publicity attendant upon complaints of breach of privilege, and to cause the House to use its penal jurisdiction more sparingly. In order to get rid of the false impression of members of the Commons as a 'privileged class', the Committee further suggested that the term 'privilege' should be replaced by that of 'rights and immunities'. But this Report has yet to be fully implemented, though Standing Orders on resolutions of the House have introduced some of the more minor recommendations. In 1977 the Committee of Privileges itself recommended that the term 'proceedings in Parliament' should be defined by legislation for the purpose of absolute privilege, but again parliamentary time has not yet been found to implement the recommendation.

VI. The Sovereignty of Parliament

It is common to say that Parliament may do anything it wishes, that it is supreme. In law this is true, and it is perhaps the most fundamental rule of British constitutional law. The only

---

5   See D. C. M. Yardley 'The House of Commons and its Privileges since the Strauss Affair' (1962) XV Parliamentary Affairs 500.

limitation is not a legal one but that of political expediency.[6] Yet parliamentary supremacy only concerns the legislative Acts of Parliament. Only these must be obeyed by courts of law, and no mere resolution or debate or answer to a question is of any importance as far as the law is concerned.[7] Statute law, therefore, is all-powerful, for it may do anything Parliament wishes; in this sense Parliament is the sovereign body in the land, provided it conforms to the necessary procedure of legislation.

In Anglo-Saxon and Norman times this was not the position. The monarch, as a result of political and factual autonomy, sometimes brought about by conquest, was supreme. He was lord of all land and dispensed all laws. When Parliament was first convened in the course of the middle ages it was with his leave, even though in fact it is possible that he might have found it politically unwise to deny its members the right so to meet. But once Parliament was established as an institution it gradually gained in power and jurisdiction, until in the seventeenth century it became necessary for it to indulge in a trial of strength with the monarchy. It is not within our present purpose to trace in any detail the fluctuations of that struggle, which at its extreme pitch led to the Civil War in the 1640s and the Bloodless Revolution of 1688–1689, but suffice it to say that by the time of that latter event Parliament was triumphant and the monarch was forced to acknowledge its supremacy. It may well be submitted that what had taken place was in fact a political revolution, and that in law nothing could wrest the power of the monarch from him but his own voluntary surrender. This may be so, and the Stuart Kings were not prepared to make such a surrender, but Parliament found the ultimate solution in 1688 by getting rid of the reigning monarch, James II, assuming supreme power, and inviting two new monarchs, William III and Mary II, to occupy the throne jointly, providing they agreed to acknowledge the supremacy of Parliament. In this way the positions were reversed, and the new monarchs reigned by leave

---

6 For a stimulating account of this principle see H. W. R. Wade 'The Basis of Legal Sovereignty' [1955] Cambridge Law Journal 172. See, however, the reference to the European Convention on Human Rights, below p 40.

7 See eg the stand taken by the Court of Queen's Bench in *Stockdale v Hansard*, cited in note 19, p 28, above.

of Parliament. In theory there are still a large number of royal prerogatives which may be exercised without recourse to the consent of Parliament, and these will be examined in the next chapter, but there is no doubt that any Parliament has the power, if it should so wish, to alter or abolish any such prerogatives which it finds uncongenial, providing such alteration or abolition is carried out by an Act of Parliament and in no other way.

The most important instrument which gave evidence of this newly won sovereignty of Parliament was the Bill of Rights 1689. In origin this was not in fact a statute at all, for it was drawn up at a time when James II had fled the country and no monarch reigned, but William and Mary had to agree to its provisions before Parliament would allow them to assume the throne. Thus no royal assent could be given to the Bill of Rights until it had already taken effect. Its juridical status was validated retrospectively by the Crown and Parliament Recognition Act 1689. A corresponding measure to the Bill of Rights for Scotland was the Claim of Right 1689. As a matter of historical fact, Parliament and William reached an amicable agreement, but there is no doubt that Parliament held the whip hand in the negotiations, for it had a throne to give away, but only on its own terms. In particular the Bill of Rights destroyed the power of any monarch to suspend the operation of a law, or to dispense with it in any individual instance, save where such dispensation had not been 'assumed and exercised of late', a loophole by which the prerogative right of pardon was preserved. Again the sole power to levy taxation was finally vested in Parliament, after what had been a long-drawn out struggle, thus re-embodying and expanding the principle that taxation requires the *consent* of the tax-payers (as now represented by Parliament), which was orginally included in Magna Carta 1215.[8] It is this control of the national purse-strings which has made Parliament's position so secure today.

It may be possible to say that the ultimate real power in any

---

8 Magna Carta was not in fact a statute in the sense that is meant today, for it merely set out the demands of the barons to which King John was forced to assent at Runnymede. Nevertheless it has always been treated as having the force and authority of a statute, both by the courts and by Parliament. It therefore must come within the confines of the fundamental law of the land which it is our purpose to discuss in this book.

nation rests in its people, who, at least in theory, control their representatives. We might say that a new nation arose in 1689, vesting its greatest power in Parliament, and that a political revolution occurred in 1688–1689, just as it had occurred in 1066 and several times in Lancastrian and Yorkist times, when the identity of the monarch was changed after resort to force. Whatever the cause, from the new order stemmed the new law. Thus our modern constitutional system and law dates from 1689. This we must accept, but the Jacobites would have been the rightful claimants to the throne if it had not been for the Revolution.

Since Parliament from that time has possessed supreme power, it follows naturally that it should be able to retain this power. It is for this reason that Parliament is said not to be able to bind its successors. Although Parliament may pass a statute in, say, 1985, by which it can enact some completely new law, yet it is still within the power of Parliament ten years later, or even only six months later, to abolish or alter that law in any way it thinks fit by a later statute, and such alteration, amendment or abolition may even take place by implication from the later enactments, if it is inconsistent with the former.[9] Perhaps the most striking example of Parliament's power to repeal former enactments is provided by the Irish Free State Constitution Act 1922, which severed that part of Ireland which is now the Republic of Ireland from the rest of the United Kingdom in flagrant violation of the Act of Union with Ireland 1800, which had declared the union of the two Kingdoms of Great Britain and Ireland to be 'for ever'. The 1800 Act also provided for the permanent establishment of the United Church of England and Ireland, yet the Church of Ireland was disestablished by the Irish Church Act 1869. It may be that the provision in the Northern Ireland Constitution Act 1973, s 1, that no part of Northern Ireland may cease to be part of Her Majesty's dominions and of the United Kingdom 'without the consent of the majority of the people of Northern Ireland voting in a poll held for the purposes of this section' would be equally ineffective to prevent such severance if ever the Westminster Parliament were determined to carry it through.

---

9   As was held in *Vauxhall Estates Ltd v Liverpoool Corpn* [1932] 1 KB 733, followed by the Court of Appeal in *Ellen Street Estates Ltd v Minister of Health* [1934] 1 KB 590.

In 1971 Salmon LJ put the position graphically in a case in which a Mr Blackburn failed to persuade the Court of Appeal to grant a declaration that the United Kingdom application to join the European Community was illegal because it would be an 'irreversible partial surrender of the Sovereignty of the Crown in Parliament'. Salmon LJ said: 'As to Parliament, in the present state of the law, it can enact, amend and repeal any legislation it pleases'.[10] On the other hand, Lord Denning MR in the same case put the practical realities of the issue into perspective. He said: 'We have all been brought up to believe that, in legal theory, one Parliament cannot bind another and that no Act is irreversible. But legal theory does not always march alongside political reality. Take the Statute of Westminster 1931, which takes away the power of Parliament to legislate for the Dominions. Can anyone imagine that Parliament could or would reverse that Statute? Take the Acts which have granted independence to the Dominions and territories overseas. Can anyone imagine that Parliament could or would reverse these laws and take away their independence? Most clearly not. Freedom once given cannot be taken away. Legal theory must give way to practical politics'.[11]

At this stage it might well be asked whether the Parliament Acts 1911 and 1949 have the effect of binding Parliament for the future as to its procedure in the passage of certain types of statute. But again the answer must be in the negative, for it is perfectly feasible that Parliament should one day abolish or amend that legislation. Parliament may always at any time legislate for the alteration of the procedure or composition of itself, and the Life Peerages Act 1958 and the Peerage Act 1963, mentioned above, are good illustrations of the application of this truth. It is important, however, to remember that in each case it must act by the composition and according to the procedure which may happen to be legally in force at the time, otherwise it would be possible for some impostor assembly to call itself the true Parliament of the realm. This, after all, is why the courts will not recognise the validity of a mere resolution of either House as law. Nevertheless the internal procedure of each House (as opposed to the relationship between the two Houses) is

---

10   *Blackburn v A-G* [1971] 1 WLR 1037 at 1041.
11   Ibid at 1040.

outside the purview of the courts, for it is within the privileges of the Houses, as has been pointed out above, to declare whether or not the proper procedure applicable in any event has been followed. As Lord Campbell once said, 'All that a Court of Justice can do is to look to the Parliament roll: if from that it should appear that a Bill has passed both Houses and received the Royal Assent, no Court of Justice can enquire into the mode in which it was introduced into Parliament, nor into what was done previous to its introduction, or what passed in Parliament during its progress in its various stages through both Houses'.[12]

Yet the power of the courts to interpret Acts can sometimes be used in effect to thwart the intentions of Parliament, though the courts do not overtly admit this. Thus in *Anisminic Ltd v Foreign Compensation Commission*[13] the House of Lords was faced with a statutory provision that a decision of the Commission 'shall not be called in question in any court of law'. Yet the Lords held that a determination by the Commission made ultra vires was void, and therefore not a decision at all, so that the court was perfectly free to set it aside. Perhaps this only illustrated how the British doctrine of parliamentary sovereignty is always dependent upon the acquiescence of the courts in it, and shows that it will only remain so long as the courts allow it to remain.

There is, in fact, a great deal of dispute among jurists as to whether Parliament, though always unfettered in area of legislative jurisdiction, may find itself bound as to the manner and form in which it may legislate. For example, would Parliament be bound by any radical change it might make in its composition, such as by abolishing the House of Lords (as was actually stated in the Preamble to the Parliament Act 1911 to be Parliament's future intention)? Again, it is far from clear whether the undoubtedly sovereign legislature, Parliament, must always remain in its present form. Is it necessary in law for Parliament to be composed of the monarch, the Lords and the Commons, or can the three component parts be differently named and formed, or be reduced in number, as has occurred in New Zealand? Could the monarchy be abolished legally, and a

---

12   *Edinburgh & Dalkeith Rly Co v Wauchope* (1842) 8 Cl & Fin 710. See also more recently the unanimous decision of the House of Lords in *British Railways Board v Pickin* [1974] AC 765, [1974] 1 All ER 609.
13   [1969] 2 AC 147, [1969] 1 All ER 208.

president or head of state put in the place of the monarch? Or would Parliament be bound by any repeal of the Bill of Rights 1689, and fresh subordination of itself to the monarch? A legislative organ is of course necessary in any modern state, if chaos is to be avoided, but it is far from clear whether the British Parliament's legal power to change the law and to legislate upon constitutional matters also includes the power to abolish or change itself radically for the future. The problem will never be solved because any such change would depend for its validity upon the continued support or otherwise of the people, a political and not a legal factor; and jurists would still argue as to whether the new order came into being by law or by political revolution. The past precedents, which include the abdication of sovereignty by the Parliaments of England and Scotland in favour of the new Parliament of Great Britain in 1706, and by the Parliament of Great Britain in favour of the new Parliament of the United Kingdom in 1800, are equally unhelpful for this reason.[14]

After a decade of negotiations the United Kingdom joined the European Community on 1 January 1973 as a result of the European Communities Act 1972, implementing the Treaty of Accession signed in 1971. The Community in fact consists of three communities in number, the European Coal and Steel Community (ECSC), the European Economic Community (EEC), and the European Atomic Energy Community (Euratom), but they share the same institutions. These are the European Parliament; the European Court of Justice; the Council of Ministers, consisting of one member of the

---

14 For further reading and the opposing views upon this problem, the following selection of materials might be studied: H. W. R. Wade 'The Basis of Legal Sovereignty' (1955) CLJ 172; H. R. Gray 'The Sovereignty of Parliament Today' (1953–1954) 10 University of Toronto LJ 54; T. B. Smith *Studies Critical and Comparative* (1962) p 1; R. F. V. Heuston *Essays in Constitutional Law* (2nd edn, 1964) Ch 1; G. Marshall *Parliamentary Sovereignty and the Commonwealth* (1957) Pt III and Appendices I–III; A. V. Dicey *Introduction to the Study of the Law of the Constitution* (10th edn, by E. C. S. Wade) Introduction and Pt 1; Sir W. Ivor Jennings *The Law and the Constitution* (5th edn, 1959) Ch IV; Sir D. L Keir and F. H. Lawson *Cases in Constitutional Law* (6th edn, 1979), Pt 1; M, A. Fazal 'Entrenched Rights and Parliamentary Sovereignty' (1974) PL 295; O. Hood Phillips 'Self-Limitation by the United Kingdom Parliament' (1975) 2 Hastings Constitutional LQ 443; G. Winterton 'The British Grundnorm: Parliamentary Supremacy Re-examined' (1976) 92 LQR 591; P. Mirfield, 'Can the House of Lords Lawfully be Abolished?' (1979) 95 LQR 37; G. Winterton 'Is the House of Lords Immortal?' 95 LQR 386.

government of each member state; and the Commission, consisting of several leading personalities, who must be nationals of member states, although not more than two members may have the same nationality, and all of whom are chosen for their 'general competence and indisputable independence'. The European Parliament (which up to 1979 consisted of members of the national Parliaments nominated by those Parliaments, but which with effect from 1979 has consisted of members elected directly by the electorates in the member states)[15] has no real legislative power. But it must be consulted on all important acts of the Community, and the Commission, which is the executive organ of the Community, is responsible to the Parliament and may be compelled to resign by a vote of censure. The Parliament has no similar control, however, over the Council of Ministers, which is the essential decision-making body of the Community, assisted in all its work by the Commission. According to Community law, therefore, national Parliaments and members of the European Parliament lose their control over matters entrusted by the Treaty to the Council. The Commission, in its function as executive organ, may make *recommendations* to member states, which are not of binding obligation, but it may also make *decisions*, which are binding upon named addressees, *directives*, which are binding in substance but leave to each member state its choice as to how to enforce them, and *regulations* which, sometimes subject to prior approval by the Council, are directly applicable in each member state. The more important directives and regulations, however, are normally made by the Council, rather than the Commission.

Although the major purpose of the Community is economic, it is clear that the powers of the Community organs not only render it necessary in fact for United Kingdom law to conform in some respects with the laws of its European partners, but also make it likely that a certain amount of law will become directly applicable in the United Kingdom from time to time without having been through the normal legislative process in the United Kingdom Parliament. Each House of the Westminster Parliament has established a Select Committee to examine such laws. Inter alia these committees make recommendations as to any amendment of United Kingdom law which may be desirable.

---

15   This provision has been brought into force in the United Kingdom by the European Assembly Elections Act 1978.

Does this mean that our Parliament has surrendered some portion of its sovereignty in favour of the Community institutions? Of course Parliament will undoubtedly usually want to do its best to conform with Community legislation, but successive Lord Chancellors have stated that it would remain within the power of Parliament to repeal by a subsequent Act any former Act applying a treaty which had been made. Under the powers enacted by the Referendum Act 1975, the first national consultative referendum was held throughout the United Kingdom, in which the electorate were asked to vote 'Yes' or 'No' to a question whether the United Kingdom should stay in the European Community. In the event there was a convincing majority for the answer 'Yes'. But the very asking of the question suggests that a contrary vote might have led to a later Bill to repeal the European Communities Act 1972. It may be that a specific Act passed later by the United Kingdom Parliament which is directly in conflict with Community legislation would have to be followed by British courts. Sorting out the result of such a clash would seem to be a political, rather than legal, matter for the government, and it may well result in later amending United Kingdom legislation. However it has now been made clear in recent court decisions that the provision in section 2(4) of the European Communities Act 1972 directing the courts to apply Community laws has the effect of precluding them from applying any earlier municipal law which is inconsistent with Community law.[16] Thus in *Macarthys Ltd v Smith*[17] the rules of Community law entitling women to equal pay with men were held by the Court of Appeal to be applicable in preference to inconsistent provisions in the Equal Pay Act 1970. Yet this very primacy of Community law is the result of the provisions of the European Communities Act 1972, which could always be repealed or amended by a later Act of Parliament. So

16 And see F. M. Auburn 'Trends in Comparative Constitutional Law' (1972) 35 MLR 129; D. G. T. Williams 'The Constitution of the United Kingdom' [1972B] CLJ 266; cf F. A. Trindade 'Parliamentary Sovereignty and the Primacy of European Community Law' (1972) 35 MLR 375; Sir Leslie Scarman 'The Law of Establishment in the European Economic Community' (1973) 24 Northern Ireland LQ 61; E. Ellis 'Parliamentary Supremacy After a Decade of EEC Membership' (1982) 7 Holdsworth LR 105; O. Hood Phillips *Constitutional and Administrative Law* (6th edn, 1978), pp 98–99.
17 [1981] QB 180, [1981] 1 All ER 111.

far as basic constitutional law is concerned, therefore, entry to the European Community, though envisaged as the first stage in a process of possible European political integration, is in itself not so fundamental a change as it may seem at first sight.

In 1966 the United Kingdom Government accepted the competence of the European Commission of Human Rights, as laid down by the European Convention on Human Rights, signed in 1950. This enables the legality of a United Kingdom Act of Parliament to be challenged before the Commission by any private individual. There is thus now the possibility of some external, though not internal, judicial review of United Kingdom Acts.[18]

A final word should be said about the status of parliamentary sovereignty in Scotland, for although it is beyond question for England, Wales and Northern Ireland, it has been doubted in a case in Scotland so far as that country is concerned. In that case, *MacCormick v Lord Advocate'*,[19] the use by Queen Elizabeth of the numeral 'II' was disputed, primarily for the very commonsense reason that although Elizabeth I had been Queen of England she had never been Queen of Scotland, and that there had never before been a Queen of Scotland known by that name. The use of the numeral ever since the Queen's accession in 1952 had been authorised by the Royal Titles Act 1953, for that statute allowed Queen Elizabeth to use whatever numeral she thought fit in the United Kingdom. But it was alleged that the Treaty of Union between England and Scotland declared that any law inconsistent with such of its terms as were declared in the Treaty itself (and the subsequent Acts of the Parliaments of England and Scotland) to be unalterable was void, and therefore that it forbade the use of the numeral in this way. It was ultimately held by the Court of Session in Edinburgh that the Treaty did not actually forbid the use of the numeral, and that the petitioner had in any case no legal title or interest to sue, but there were nevertheless dicta to the effect that had the 1953 Act been repugnant to the Treaty, then the later Act would have been void unless it was generally approved in Scotland. It is far from

---

18   As in *Golder v United Kingdom*, decided by the European Court of Human Rights on 21 February 1975 [1975] Yearbook of the European Convention on Human Rights 290.

19   1953 SC 396; and see similar doubts in *Gibson v Lord Advocate* 1975 SLT 134.

clear in these dicta whether the sovereign body for Scotland is really the whole people (presumably expressing their will by plebiscite, which had never before been held there), or whether it is the International Court at the Hague (though this latter suggestion is most unlikely to be correct, in view of the status of the United Kingdom as a *union*). It is not suggested that the Treaty is so fundamental as to be totally unchangeable, for statutory alterations have been made before,[20] but on those occasions the changes have never been challenged in the courts, and apparently must possess the approbation of the people. The solution to this puzzle is still unknown, though an application to the European Commission of Human Rights would now seem feasible. We may be sceptical as to the validity of the special Scots law rule today.[1] At any rate with this possible exception for Scotland,[2] the principle of parliamentary sovereignty in the United Kingdom remains one of the most basic tenets of our constitutional law.

FURTHER READING

Sir William R. Anson *The Law and Custom of the Constitution* Vol 1: Parliament (5th edn, by M. L. Gwyer, 1922)

Sir Thomas Erskine May *The Law, Privileges, Proceedings and Usages of Parliament* (20th edn, by Sir Charles Gordon, 1983)

Sir W. Ivor Jennings *Parliament* (3rd edn, 1969)

Sir Gilbert Campion *An Introduction to the Procedure of the House of Commons* (1947)

G. Marshall *Parliamentary Sovereignty and the Commonwealth* (1957)

T. B. Smith 'The Union of 1707 as Fundamental Law' [1957] PL 99, reproduced in *Studies Critical and Comparative* (1962) p 1.

A. H. Hanson and H. V. Wiseman 'The Use of Committees by the House of Commons' [1959] PL 277

Kilmuir, Rt Hon the Viscount *The Law of Parliamentary Privilege* (pamphlet) (1959)

---

20 Eg by the Universities (Scotland) Act 1853, which enacted that professors at Scottish universities need no longer be members of the Presbyterian Church of Scotland.

1 And see S. A. de Smith, *Constitutional and Administrative Law* (4th edn, 1981) p 82.

2 One further possible, though doubtful, exception is provided by s 4 of the Statute of Westminster 1931. For this, see Chapter 13, below.

P. S. R. F. Mathijsen *A Guide to European Community Law* (3rd edn, 1980)
D. Lasok and J. W. Bridge *An Introduction to the Law and Institutions of the European Community* (3rd edn, 1982)

Chapter 3

The Executive

The executive is the organ of state which is responsible for carrying out the law and performing the routine administration of the country. Up till the seventeenth century, as has been pointed out above in Chapter 2, the authority for this exercise of power derived from its own strength and ability to coerce opposition, but since that time it has exercised its powers with the authority of Parliament. Traditionally the monarch is the all-powerful part of the executive, but from earliest times he has acted with advisers, and since the subordination of the executive power to that of Parliament these advisers have become so much more important that in fact they are now the active members of the executive, while the monarch is usually only informed of decisions made and actions carried out or to be carried out. An example of this principle in practice is the custom of the Chancellor of the Exchequer to inform the monarch of his Budget proposals each year on the day before he is due to introduce them into the House of Commons. But the executive is still in law referred to as 'the Crown', and this has become a collective term to cover not merely the monarch but the whole body of his advisers and their servants. The Crown thus symbolises the central government. It is correct to classify the Prime Minister as a part of the Crown, and just as correct so to place the most junior of inland revenue officials and all members of the armed forces.

For convenience the component part of the Crown or executive may be stated to be:

1 the monarch,
2 his ministers,
3 the central government departments, staffed by the civil service, and
4 the armed forces.

Cutting across this division, as far as 1, 2 and 3 above are concerned, is the Privy Council, which is also part of the Crown. Its nature will be explained in due course in this chapter.

I. The Monarch

The monarch is the King or Queen Regnant for the time being, and holds the position of head of state. Throughout this book the term 'monarch' is used to describe the person of the head of state in the United Kingdom, for it is thought to be more definitive than 'King' or 'Queen', which may appear to refer to a particular monarch, or 'sovereign', which may be confused with parliamentary sovereignty. Succession to the monarchy is hereditary under the terms of the Act of Settlement 1700, as amended by the Act of Union with Scotland 1706, the Act of Union with Ireland 1800, and His Majesty's Declaration of Abdication Act 1936. Under these statutes the heirs of Sophia, Electress of Hanover, who was a granddaughter of King James I, were to succeed to the throne according to rules similar in most respects to those governing feudal descent of land, provided that no heir may succeed to the throne unless he or she is in communion with the Church of England. The present Monarch is Queen Elizabeth II. Provision is made by the Regency Acts 1937–1953 for the appointment of a regent if the monarch should be below the age of 18 years or seriously ill, and for counsellors of state if the monarch should be sent from the realm.

II. The Ministers of the Crown

The monarch's advisers are often collectively termed 'the government', though this phrase is misleading, for in theory the whole of the Crown is the government. They are, however, the most vital members of the government, for they are responsible for the formulation of executive policy. As the Crown carries out its functions under the control of Parliament, it has become a convention of the constitution that the ministers should be drawn from the political party with a majority in the House of Commons, or occasionally from any coalition of parties which hold such a majority. The continuation in power of any particular government depends upon the continued support of Parliament, or, more particularly, of the Commons, and thus the legislature and the executive are closely dovetailed in the British Constitution. The monarch has the right to choose his Prime Minister, who will in turn choose the other ministers with the approval of the monarch. This right of the monarch is, however, of little real importance, as the continuation in office of the ministers will depend upon the support of a majority in the Commons which is unlikely to be forthcoming unless they are acceptable to such a majority. The stated practice of the Labour Party is to elect a leader who alone would be supported by the party as Prime Minister, and in 1965 the Conservative Party adopted a somewhat similar practice.

The Prime Minister, with the consent of the monarch, usually appoints to ministerial office members of either House of Parliament. Most of the ministers will be members of the Commons,[1] and the rest by convention sit in the Lords. In the rare case of the Prime Minister appointing as minister someone who does not sit in either House it is usual for that person to be created a peer. It is customary that the heads of the more important ministries should be members of the Commons, so that they may explain or defend themselves and their policies in the House where the elected representatives of the people are assembled. It now appears to be a convention for the Prime Minister himself to be a member of the Commons, rather than of the Lords,[2] and the Chancellor of the Exchequer must perforce sit in the lower House, which alone is concerned with financial affairs. It is not our present purpose to provide a detailed list of the ministers, for such a list would contain the names of over 100 different offices. A few examples of those at present in existence should suffice. Among the more important offices are those of Lord Chancellor, Chancellor of the Exchequer, Secretary of State for Foreign and Commonwealth Affairs, and Home

---

1 The House of Commons Disqualification Act 1975 limits the number of ministers who may sit in the Commons to 95.

2 Most writers assert that this practice has the status of a convention, as the last Prime Minister who sat in the Lords was Lord Salisbury (1895–1902). It may be noted that the Earl of Home was appointed Prime Minister in 1963 while a member of the Lords, and he did not renounce his peerage under the Peerage Act 1963 until four days later. He was then a member of neither House of Parliament for some two weeks until he had successfully fought a by-election for a seat in the Commons.

Secretary. All such ministers are the heads of different government departments, which in the case of the offices just quoted are respectively the Lord Chancellor's Department, the Exchequer, the Foreign and Commonwealth Office and the Home Office. Among lesser ministers are, eg, the Attorney-General, Ministers of State in various departments (who may be regarded roughly as second ministers in such departments), Parliamentary Secretaries and Under-Secretaries of State. Although all such officials are members of the government, a small inner group of the more important ministers is called the Cabinet, which meets frequently under the chairmanship of the Prime Minister or, if he or she is absent, a deputy appointed by the Prime Minister, and very probably formulates most government policy, only consulting junior ministers as and when it seems appropriate or desirable. It is impossible to say with any certainty what does take place in Cabinet meetings, as they are very secret and no publication of their transactions is allowed for many years. Again, the government normally provides a display of unanimity concerning its policies, both in Parliament and outside. Any disagreement is ironed out in private, or else, as sometimes occurs, any minister who cannot accept the majority view will resign from office.

The one major exception to this rule was provided in 1975 when the government consciously permitted ministers to express different views, and even to campaign actively for them, before the referendum in June upon whether or not the United Kingdom should remain a member of the European Community. It is generally considered that future governments will not wish to follow this precedent, though the government allowed a free vote in the Commons for its members on the European Assembly Elections Bill in 1977.

III. The Central Government Departments

All the Departments of the Crown which are concerned with the government of the country are termed Central Government Departments, and each is headed either by a minister or, in the case of non-political departments, such as that concerned with inland revenue or with customs and excise, by a permanent head or commissioner. Although the ministers will change whenever a government changes, the permanent officials will not, and even in the political departments there will always be an official, designated as Permanent Secretary, at the head of the permanent staff, who will see that his minister's policy is carried out. The permanent staff are all members of the civil service, a body of permanent Crown servants recruited into the service as a career, though legally only holding office at the pleasure of the Crown.

As in the case of the different ministers, it is not intended to detail all the Central Government Departments. The ambit of the work of most will be self-evident, as in the case of, for example, the Ministry of Defence, the Foreign and Common-wealth Office, and the Department of the Environment. Perhaps a word should be said here about the departments of the Lord Chancellor and of the Law Officers, as these are of particular interest to lawyers. The Lord High Chancellor of Great Britain is Keeper of the Great Seal and presides over the House of Lords both as a legislative assembly and as a final court of appeal.[3] With the help of his department he selects all puisne judges of the High Court, Circuit Judges and Recorders, who are then formally appointed by the Crown on his advice, and he appoints and removes all Justices of the Peace, except those in the Duchy of Lancaster who are appointed and removed by the Chancellor of the Duchy of Lancaster.[4] In addition he is responsible, with the aid of his department, and of his Law Reform Committee and the English Law Commissioners,[5] for advising on questions of law reform. The Law Officers are the Attorney-General and Solicitor-General for England and Wales, and the Lord Advocate and Solicitor-General for Scotland. The English Law Officers are usually members of the House of Commons, and the Scottish Law Officers may be, though in recent years one or other of the Scottish Law Officers has often been a member of the House of Lords, and sometimes one of them has been a member of neither House. Their responsibilities differ slightly,

---

3 On this subject see Chapter 4, below.
4 The nature of these various judicial offices will be explained in Chapter 4, below.
5 The Law Commissions Act 1965 establishes two Commissions, one for England and Wales, and the other for Scotland, responsible respectively to the Lord Chancellor and to the Lord Advocate and the Secretary of State for Scotland, and with the duty to review the law with a view to its systematic development and reform, including preparation for codification and the repeal of obsolete and unnecessary Acts.

but in the main they represent the Crown in civil litigation in England (including Wales) and they may prosecute in both England and Scotland in criminal cases of great importance or gravity, especially murder cases. The English Law Officers hold positions as the head of the Bar, and thus have some authority in questions of professional etiquette, though most questions of this kind are dealt with by the Senate of the Inns of Court and the Bar in London or by the Faculty of Advocates in Edinburgh. The Head of the Scottish Bar is the Dean of the Faculty of Advocates. The Law Officers advise other Government Departments on points of law. They or their deputies may intervene in litigation where the interests of the public would require such a course to be taken, for they are the representatives of the public interest where public rights are at stake.

All Government Departments will have powers and duties conferred upon them by Acts of Parliament, and these may in turn be supplemented by powers acquired under the Royal Prerogative, which will be examined later in this chapter. Although in the past it was more useful for statutes to confer powers upon the monarch, it is now common to find statutes conferring such duties or powers upon ministers or departments direct and by name. In view of the majority support in the Commons which any government should be able to command, and which it must command in order to remain an effective government, it may be that the government does from time to time have a tendency to dictate to Parliament by telling it what it intends to do and relying on its party majority to carry through its proposals. Thus, although Parliament still in theory maintains the whip-hand over the executive, in practice the reverse may sometimes be more true. Where this is so the result may sometimes be regrettable, but it cannot be denied that inevitably it gives rise to strong government in a way unknown in, for example, France for many decades, at least up till the establishment of the Fifth Republic in 1958, for there the multiplication of political parties led to the necessity of a succession of coalition governments. Although there is a danger of the British government acting in a highhanded way occasionally, yet the legal sovereignty of Parliament is always present, and no government would be able to try the patience or conscience of its own customary supporters too far without finding an incipient rebellion on its hands.

IV. The Privy Council

The Privy Council has a far longer history than the present Cabinet or government system. It dates from Anglo-Saxon and early Norman origins, and was an earlier body of advisers of the monarch. Although the present Cabinet has really usurped this ancient position of the Privy Council, the older body has never become entirely obsolete, and it still has some important functions. Appointment to the Council is still technically by the monarch himself, although membership is now partly conventional and partly arranged according to the wishes of the government of the day, with the one distinction that members are appointed for life. The conventional members are:

a the Lord President of the Council, who normally presides at any of the Council's meetings, and who is in any case a member of the government for the time being;

b the Archbishops of Canterbury and York;

c the Speaker of the House of Commons;

d all present and former Cabinet ministers, but not other members of the government; and

e the Lords of Appeal in Ordinary, the Lords Justices of Appeal, the Lord Chief Justice, the Master of the Rolls and the President of the Family Division of the High Court.

Other persons who from time to time attain the rank of Privy Councillor, as and when the monarch or the government decide on such appointment, are usually leading statesmen from other Commonwealth countries, or distinguished persons from any walk of life.

The purposes of the Privy Council today are several, but it only meets as a full body (about 300 Privy Councillors are usually living at any one time) on the death of the monarch, when it will make all arrangements for the funeral, accession and coronation that may be necessary. This meeting of the Council is sometimes known as an Accession Council. Otherwise the meetings of the Privy Council are always in small bodies or as committees. The most important function is that of making Proclamations or Orders in Council. Proclamations may be made under the Royal Prerogative, to be explained in the next few pages, usually on the advice of the Prime Minister. Orders in Council are largely made under statutory powers, and will be considered more fully in Chapter 10 below. Committees of the Council sit for various purposes, such as to deal with constitutional issues concerning universities and colleges, to direct research in certain fields, and to hear appeals from other countries within the Commonwealth.[6]

V. The Armed Forces

All members of the Royal Navy, Army and Royal Air Force[7] are servants of the Crown, and thus these services may be regarded as being parts of the Crown. The powers of the armed forces and their members are controlled partly by Acts of Parliament direct and partly through certain prerogative powers of the Crown. All members of the armed forces are dismissable by the Crown at will, and at common law no action will lie at the suit of a serviceman against the Crown for arrears of pay, or for wrongful dismissal or the refusal of a pension after service ceases,[8] unless such a pension has been fixed by statute.

VI. The Position of the Police Forces[9]

Although policemen have the duty to enforce the criminal law, and have wide powers to arrest, they are not servants of the Crown.[10] The Police Act 1964, however, provides that a Chief Constable shall be vicariously liable for torts committed by constables under his direction and control. All police officers belong to one of the separate and independent police forces of the country. These are the county and area police forces, the City of

---

6   In the Judicial Committee of the Privy Council: see Chapter 4, below.
7   This is not an exclusive list, for these services are now divided up in many ways. The principles cited in this section cover all members of the regular armed forces, including, for example, the Royal Marines and the women's services. The various reserve and auxiliary forces are also included. The Home Guard, which no longer exists as an armed force, was in the same position, and doubtless would be again if ever it were reconstituted.
8   See eg *Grant v Secretary of State for India* (1877) 2 CPD445. The position has not been affected by the Crown Proceedings Act 1947, which will be discussed in Chapter 11, below.
9   This section deals only with the position in England and Wales: that for Scotland and Northern Ireland is somewhat different.
10   *A-G for New South Wales v Perpetual Trustee Co* [1955] AC 457, [1955] 1 All ER 846.

London Police Force, and the Metropolitan Police Force. Only the last is truly controlled by the Crown as to matters of policy etc, for it is under the direct control of the Home Secretary, and the Crown appoints its Commissioner on the advice of the Home Secretary. Elsewhere the Home Secretary has the power to regulate concerning national conditions of service, which include wage rates, uniforms to be worn, pensions etc. The Police Act 1964 also gives him power to call for a report upon any specific matter from a Chief Constable, to call upon a local police authority to require a Chief Constable, or his assistant or deputy, to retire in the interests of efficiency, and to cause a local inquiry to be held into the policing of any area. There has been a marked tendency in recent years towards amalgamation of more and more separate forces, which may well lead to increased efficiency and cooperation, and the Home Secretary's powers to instigate amalgamation were increased by the 1964 Act. Each police force is under the control of a police authority, consisting as to two-thirds of members of constituent local councils and as to one-third of magistrates for the constituent areas. The Chief Constable in each case is appointed by the relevant police authority. The head of the City of London Police Force is a Commissioner appointed by the Court of Common Council of the City of London Corporation.[11] Nevertheless the Home Secretary maintains certain other indirect control of all the forces, because his approval is necessary for the appointment of any Chief Constable (or Commissioner of the City of London Police) to become effective. The granting of such approval is more than a mere formality, and in recent years approval has several times been refused in order to prevent a local man becoming Chief Constable: in the interest of preventing corruption etc. it is thought better that a stranger should be appointed. In addition, any constable or officer who feels himself aggrieved by certain decisions of his local police authority may appeal to the Home Secretary, who has the power to alter such decisions if he sees fit.

Grants are made from the Exechequer under statutory powers to local authorities for various services, including help for financing the local police forces, and it would be possible, though very rare, for any Home Secretary to exert pressure upon a local

---

11 See Chapter 12, below.

police authority by moving to suspend or reduce such payments for particular reasons.[12] Thus the government may maintain some control over the police of the whole country, although full control is limited to the metropolis. The Report of the Royal Commission on the Police, issued in 1962, recommended that more responsibility should be given to the central government to promote co-ordination between police forces in the work of fighting crime and dealing with traffic, and the 1964 Act has carried out these recommendations. But Dr A. L. Goodhart, in a powerful dissenting memorandum, considered that real efficiency in combating crime could only be achieved by the outright creation of a national force, regionally administered, with the Home Secretary responsible to Parliament for its proper maintenance and administration. It remains to be seen whether Dr Goodhart's more radical views will ever triumph over the trend of cautious evolution which his colleagues on the Royal Commission favoured.

The Police Act 1976 provides for the first time for the establishment of an independent Police Complaints Board which receives reports of any investigations by the police of complaints about any members of the police. The Board has the power to direct that disciplinary proceedings should be taken before a Disciplinary Tribunal consisting of the relevant Chief Officer of Police and two members of the Board.

VII. The Position of Public Corporations

It is not uncommon for a layman to believe that nationalised industries and monopolies are creatures of the government. This is not necessarily so. Wherever an industry or undertaking has been put upon a national footing, with either a complete or a partial monopoly for one body to exercise, the practice has usually been to create a public corporation by Act of Parliament or by Royal Charter. Instances are the British Broadcasting Corporation, the National Coal Board, the British Airways Corporation and the British Railways Board. These bodies are incorporated by statute and became legal entities with much the

---

12   Such grants have been withheld four times since 1945: see B. Whitaker *The Police* (1964) p 91.

same result as in the case of other companies or corporations. The government very frequently retains the power to nominate or appoint some proportion of the directors or managers of these organisations, and there is no offer of investment facilities for the general public, but they are fully liable (unless the creating statute provides otherwise, which is rare) both criminally and civilly, and they do not normally become servants or agents of the Crown. Their statutes usually provide that reports and accounts are to be submitted to Parliament every year, and in this way Parliament retains some direct control over their affairs, and may decide upon the appropriate sums of money to be voted to them for future operations. But no minister is responsible for the day-to-day running of public corporations, and this means that ministers may not be asked questions about such matters in Parliament.

VIII. The Royal Prerogative

One last topic remains to be considered in this chapter. The prerogatives of the monarch have always been recognised by the courts in much the same way as they have recognised Parliamentary privilege.[13] Blackstone referred to the royal prerogative as 'that special pre-eminence which the King hath, over and above all other persons, and out of the ordinary course of the Common law, in right of his regal dignity'.[14] But since the Bill of Rights 1689 there is little doubt that such prerogatives as remain to the Crown exist by tacit permission of Parliament. So long as Parliament continues to allow the monarch or the Crown (for most of the prerogatives are now exercised only on the advice of the monarch's ministers) to retain any prerogatives, then those prerogatives will be pre-eminent, but they could always be swept away by Act of Parliament. But since the convention of advice upon which the monarch acts leads to the placing of considerable extra power in the hands of the government of the day, it would appear very unlikely that any government party (or indeed any Opposition party, which in turn hopes to become the government party) should wish to

13 See Chapter 2, above.
14 1 Bl Comm 239.

sweep them away. Parliament does, however, occasionally abridge, modify or replace such powers by statutory powers, as, for example, for defence purposes: and one notable instance of a partial abolition of a previously existing prerogative was the passage of the Crown Proceedings Act 1947, which will be discussed in Chapter 11. In a case of 1920,[15] Dicey's definition of the royal prerogative was approved: 'the residue of discretionary or arbitrary authority, which at any given time is legally left in the hands of the Crown'.

It is difficult to find a satisfactory division of the existing prerogatives of the Crown, and it is in any case not intended to give an exhaustive list here, but perhaps the following classification will serve its purpose:

(A) PREROGATIVES WHICH AFFECT THE PERSON OF THE MONARCH OR THE STATUS OF THE CROWN

These provide for the monarch's personal immunity from legal action, that he is not affected by the general law concerning the disability of infancy, that the Crown is only to be affected by the passage of a statute if that statute concerns it expressly or must do so by necessary implication, and that on the death of one monarch his successor immediately takes office.

(B) PREROGATIVES WHICH ARE OF WIDER IMPLICATION

These may be of an executive, legislative or judicial nature, and it is convenient to divide them up accordingly.

(i) Legislative.   The monarch summons, prorogues and dissolves Parliament, and he also gives the royal assent to legislation. He may legislate by Order in Council or by Proclamation (as explained above) for newly conquered or ceded colonies, until he has sanctioned a constitution with a representative legislature in the colony.

The only modern instance of the royal prerogative being used to dissolve Parliament, and also to dismiss the Prime Minister and his government without the advice of the government to do so, was in Australia in 1975. There the prerogative is vested in the Governor-General, and has nothing to do in reality with the

---

15   *A-G v De Keyser's Royal Hotel Ltd* [1920] AC508, [1920] All ER Rep 80.

monarch, and it was exercised when the federal government had ceased to be able to persuade the federal parliament to pass its measures into law, and had failed either to resign or to call on the Governor-General to dissolve Parliament with a view to a general election. Such a use of prerogative power will clearly be rare, but it illustrates the kind of residuary power of the monarch which is an important safeguard in the British Constitution.

(ii) Executive. Many of these prerogatives are mere relics of past days, but the more important include the following. The monarch is technically head of all the armed forces. The monarch appoints and dismisses ministers,[16] civil servants, and officers and members of the armed forces. The monarch creates peers and confers honours. The monarch may create corporations by Royal Charter. In cases of national emergency the Crown is responsible for defence of the realm, and is the only judge of the existence of danger from external enemies.[17] The Crown may also, in time of war, requisition ships[18] and enter on private land to repel invasion,[19] although where a statute is applicable it must act under that, rather than under the prerogative power.[20] The requisitioning of ships at very short notice during the Falklands conflict in 1982 was an example of the exercise of such statutory power. In the field of foreign affairs the royal prerogative is perhaps most important of all, for it is within the prerogative to declare war, make peace or enter into treaties, all without recourse to parliamentary approval, although such approval will be required later if the rights of citizens are affected or the expenditure of public money is required. Foreign states, governments or heads of state may be recognised by the Crown, and the sending and receiving of diplomatic representatives is again within the prerogative. A certain defence, known as the defence of 'act of state', may be raised under the prerogative power. It applies in cases where the Crown has done some act in relation to a foreign state or an alien enemy anywhere, or with respect to friendly aliens ie citizens of

16 The monarch, as has been observed above, still appoints the Prime Minister personally, but not the other ministers.

17 *R v Hampden* (1637) 3 State Tr 826.

18 *The Broadmayne* [1916] P64 at 67.

19 *Case of the King's Prerogative in Saltpetre* (1907) 12 Co Rep 12; *Burmah Oil Co v Lord Advocate* [1965] AC75, [1964] 2 All ER 348.

20 *A-G v De Keyser's Royal Hotel Ltd* [1920] AC508, [1920] All ER Rep 80.

foreign countries with which the United Kingdom is not at war) who are outside the monarch's dominions. If such foreign state, alien enemy or friendly alien not within temporary allegiance brings an action against the Crown, the defence of 'act of state' is a complete one, and the action must fail. This is also so where the act was committed by a servant of the Crown under orders, and even where the servant was not under such orders, but the Crown has chosen to 'adopt' his act retrospectively.[1] It seems, however, that no 'act of state' defence is available to the Crown in respect of acts committed by the Crown against a British subject anywhere.[2]

(iii) Judicial. The monarch is still technically the 'fountain of justice', and the fiction still exists that he is present in *his* own courts, though the judges resolved as long ago as 1607[3] that he may not give an opinion on any case. In theory he normally prosecutes, and all writs are in his name. But it should be remembered that the judges of superior courts no longer hold office at the monarch's pleasure.[4] Again the monarch possesses the prerogative of mercy, in that convicted persons may be pardoned or reprieved by royal command, exercised through the Home Secretary.

From this brief sketch it may be seen that in theory the prerogatives are numerous and wide, but very few of them are still exercised by the monarch in person and according to his own discretion, and all exist only by leave of Parliament. In their present form they are of considerable practical use to any government, and in particular the prerogatives concerning foreign affairs are well-nigh essential for the proper functioning of our relations with other states. It may be that the term 'Royal prerogative' is itself unfortunate in the modern law as it leads some students to believe that the monarch has more real power than is in fact the case. Perhaps 'residuary executive power', or some such expression, might more accurately convey the present position. But the current terminology is a natural result of a monarchical establishment. Provided that it is remembered that

---

1   *Buron v Denman* (1848) 2 Exch 167.
2   *A-G v Nissan* [1970] AC179, [1969] 1 All ER629.
3   *Prohibitions del Roy* 12 CoRep63 at 64.
4   See p 47, above, for the contrary position of Circuit Judges, Recorders and magistrates.

'the Crown' usually means the whole of the executive, confusion should be eliminated. It is worth noting that the most important part of the monarch's own personal share of the royal prerogative is also its most nebulous area of power, namely the right to advise and warn his ministers, and to be consulted and informed by them.

FURTHER READING

Sir W. Ivor Jennings *Cabinet Government* (3rd edn, 1959)
Lord MacDermott *Protection from Power under English Law* (1957) Ch 2
Final Report of the Royal Commission of the Police, 1962, Cmnd 1728
B. Whitaker *The Police* (1964)
G. Marshall *Police and Government* (1965)
T. C. Hartley and J. A. G. Griffith *Government and Law* (1975)
D. C. M. Yardley 'The Primacy of the Executive in England' (1968) XXI *Parliamentary Affairs* 155

Chapter 4

The Judiciary

Nothing more than the barest sketch of the system of courts and judges can be attempted in these pages, for the actual identity of the various courts is of little importance in the field of constitutional law. The power of the courts as a whole is what really matters in this respect, and the lawyer is entitled to expect that this power in any given instance will only be wielded by the court having the proper jurisdiction. Should the applicant for any remedy seek it in the wrong court it is the duty of such court to dismiss his application for that reason, and even if the court of first instance should fail to take this step there is always the possibility of appeal to a higher court upon this issue, or else, in the case of what are known as inferior courts, certain extra-ordinary remedies may be obtained to nullify the first proceedings. It will be noted that we are only concerned specifically with English courts in this chapter. The courts of Scotland and Northern Ireland are quite separate, as will be explained in Chapter 7 below, yet their powers as far as constitutional law is concerned are similar. It is intended in the present chapter, therefore, to consider first the constitutional position of all courts throughout the United Kingdom, and then to outline the nature of the various courts of law in England alone, the doctrine of precedent and the concept of judicial tenure. The English courts will thus be used as exemplifying a *system* which is common in all parts of the United Kingdom.

I. The Constitutional Position of the Courts

The primary function of the court is to determine the legality of various kinds of behaviour. This is not to say that it is open to any court to investigate an issue upon its own initiative. In each case it is for an individual to raise the matter as the subject of litigation in which he is involved, whether the issue is one of civil or of criminal law. In the field of criminal law most prosecution in England (the position is rather different in Scotland) is undertaken by the police or by the Department of the Director of Public Prosecutions, who is appointed by the Home Secretary to initiate prosecutions for murder and certain other crimes, under the control of the Lord Chancellor and the Attorney-General. But in some criminal cases and in civil cases of all kinds the litigation may be started by any private individual or by a corporation, as well as by the Crown. Indeed in theory it may be that the police really only undertake prosecutions as private individuals.

Once an issue has been raised in the appropriate court, it is for that court to reach its decision according to the law of the land. Not infrequently the law is regarded as certain, and the main problem in hand will be to determine the facts in the case before the court and then to apply the law to these particular facts. But sometimes there is doubt about the exact law upon a point, and it is then that the court has a discretion to make its own decision upon the nature of the legal rule involved. As has been seen above in Chapter 2, Parliament in its legislative capacity may introduce, alter or repeal any law it thinks fit, and in each case the effect will have been to formulate a new law for the future. Such law is absolutely binding upon all courts,[1] and the only discretion permitted to the courts is that of deciding how the law is to be applied to particular facts. But not all law is statutory. A large part of the law is 'common law', in the sense of having been made by the decisions of courts, according to case-precedent where statute law has not yet encroached upon the particular field of law concerned. Although it would be realistic to consider this function as being legislative, yet it is more customary to regard it as adjudicatory upon the various opinions put before the court of what the law on a particular topic may or must be. In either event such decisions may always be overriden by a later Act of Parliament. Perhaps the only way in which it is at all

---

1 Cf however the possible exception in Scots law, described at p 40, above. Northern Ireland courts are absolutely bound by Acts of the Westminster Parliament, but may declare Acts of the old Northern Ireland Parliament invalid if made outside the powers of that body or in contravention of United Kingdom legislation: see Chapter 7, below.

possible for a court effectively to express its opinion upon a statute is by interpretation of the Act when it is arguable that more than one meaning may be accorded to the wording of the Act which is in point. In one or two instances it has been known for courts to interpret statutes in such a way as in effect to flout the intention of Parliament,[2] but such instances are rare, and in any case cannot be blatant, for the bounden duty of the court is to apply the letter of the statute strictly, and in interpreting the meaning of a particular Act its only permitted object is to be able to enforce it once the meaning is discovered.

It will be seen, therefore, that the function of the courts is to discover and apply the law, and so to decide between the merits of arguments raised before them by exercising this function. The behaviour of the executive may be scrutinised by the courts upon these principles, and if necessary declared to be illegal, though certain exceptions to this general rule will be discussed later in Chapter 11. But it is never possible for the courts to question the validity of existing Acts of Parliament.[3] In this way the British Constitution differs from that of the majority of other countries of the world. Oddly enough the Constitution of the United States of America also differs upon this point from most other written constitutions, for, although article III vests the federal judicial power in the United States Supreme Court, there is no provision for any power to review legislative Acts of Congress. Yet such a reviewing power has been read into the Constitution by construction, and is now treated as beyond any doubt.[4] Any such Acts which do not conform to the provisions of the Constitution will be held invalid. In the United Kingdom all Acts of Parliament are treated as absolutely binding by the courts, regardless of whether they have any constitutional significance or not,[5] until such time as any particular Act is repealed or altered by Parliament itself in another statute.[6] Thus the courts, like all other institutions of the United Kingdom, have powers subordinate to the one most basic concept of the British Constitution, the sovereignty of Parliament.

2 See the *Anisminic* case, discussed above, p 36.
3 See, however, footnote 1, p 59. As has been noted already in Chapter 2, no court is bound by any resolution of one of the Houses of Parliament which does not amount to a statute.
4 See particularly the judgment of Chief Justice Marshall in *Marbury v Madison* (1803) 1 Cranch 137; and Learned Hand *The Bill of Rights* (1958) Lecture 1.
5 See Chapter 2, above.
6 Or else by delegated legislation: see Chapter 10, below.

II. The English Courts of Law

In this brief account it is convenient to divide the English courts into two groups, namely those which have a civil jurisdiction and those with a criminal jurisdiction.

A. CIVIL COURTS

The lowest courts in the hierarchy are the *magistrates' courts*, which have a limited jurisdiction over certain types of small civil disputes. The importance of these courts in civil cases is now, however, very minor. Most magistrates are unpaid Justices of the Peace (JPs), appointed and removable for each area by the Lord Chancellor on the advice of the Lord Lieutenant of the County (or by the Chancellor of the Duchy of Lancaster for that county). They are normally laymen, but they are assisted on points of law by the clerk of the court wherever they request his help, provided that he may never advise them on what their actual decision should be. Since 1966 there has been a short course of compulsory training for all new JPs. Appeals from magistrates' courts may be taken to the *Crown Court* or to a *Divisional Court of the High Court*, both of which courts will be described presently. If an appeal is taken to the Crown Court, a further appeal may lie to the Divisional Court later. Alternatively, the record of a case may be removed for review by the Divisional Court under the procedure of certiorari, which will be explained in Chapter 11.

County Courts have existed since 1846, when they were originally created by the County Courts Act. Their jurisdiction has been increased in scope several times since then, and now covers all types of minor civil disputes, with only a few exceptions. The factor which determines whether a dispute is minor or major is normally the pecuniary value of the subject-matter in dispute. Ordinary cases of contract or tort up to the value of £5000 in dispute are usually brought in the County Court, though in other cases concerning, for example, recovery of land or probate, the limit is higher or lower according to the statutory provisions in force.[7] The judges

---

7 The most recent statutes are the County Courts Act 1959, the County Courts (Jurisdiction) Act 1963, the Administration of Justice Act 1969, the Courts Act 1971, and the Administration of Justice Act 1982.

appointed for County Courts are known as Circuit Judges, and they are appointed and removable by the monarch on the advice of the Lord Chancellor. A jury may sit if either party wishes it where the sum claimed exceeds £5, though such a jury is rarely called upon in practice. In London the County Court retains the name of *Mayor's and City of London Court*. Appeals from decisions of County Courts lie, except in certain rare types of case, to the *Court of Appeal*, which is described below.

All other civil cases are heard in the *High Court of Justice*, which, together with the *Crown Court*, is part of the *Supreme Court of Judicature*, originally created by the Judicature Act 1873 and now governed by the Courts Act 1971 and the Supreme Court Act 1981. The High Court is divided into the *Chancery Division*, the *Queen's Bench Division* and the *Family Division*, each dealing for the most part with subjects for which it is best suited, although there is no strict rule that a case of any particular kind may only be brought in the appropriate Division and in no other. Generally speaking, however, most equity disputes appear in the Chancery Division, the primary business of the Family Division is implicit in its name, and the remainder of civil litigation appears in the Queen's Bench Division. Jury trial is now unusual in civil cases in the High Court, although it is still possible in certain types of dispute. The judges of the High Court are puisne Judges, appointed by the Crown on the advice of the Lord Chancellor. In addition, the Lord Chancellor is in strict law the president of the whole High Court and, more particularly, of the Chancery Division, of which latter Division the Master of the Rolls, appointed by the Crown on the advice of the Prime Minister, is another member; but in practice neither will sit in the High Court. The Vice-Chancellor is the formal Vice-President of the Chancery Division, and there is a President of the Family Division, while the Lord Chief Justice of England presides over the Queen's Bench Division. These latter judges are appointed by the Crown on the advice of the Prime Minister. For the hearing of cases at first instance the judges sit singly, and it is therefore usual in the High Court (and in the sittings of two or three judges in the Court of Appeal, discussed below) to find several judges sitting in different 'courts' at the same time, each exercising the full power of the court. But for certain special purposes, such as the hearing of appeals from magistrates' courts, the judges of the High Court may sit in benches of two or three as a *Divisional Court* of one or other of the Divisions, normally of the Queen's Bench Division. The High Court usually sits in London, but it may also sit in other parts of the country.

Appeals from the High Court or the County Court lie to the *Civil Division of the Court of Appeal*, the judges of which are the Master of the Rolls and the Lords Justices of Appeal, appointed by the Crown on the advice of the Prime Minister. They normally sit as a bench of two or three. The Lord Chancellor, the Lord Chief Justice, the President of the Family Division, the Vice-Chancellor and the Lords of Appeal in Ordinary, are also members of the court, but in practice the president is the Master of the Rolls and only the Lords Justices normally sit with him.

The ultimate court of Appeal in civil cases from English, Scottish or Northern Ireland courts is the *House of Lords*, where the judges are the Lords of Appeal in Ordinary ('Law Lords'), appointed by the Crown on the advice of the Prime Minister, who must have a quorum of three, but frequently sit as a group of five, and occasionally even of seven. Lay peers may not, by convention, sit when the House is hearing appeals, but any peers who hold or have held high judicial office may sit. The president is the Lord Chancellor. The House normally hears appeals in a committee room, and not in the legislative chamber. In certain special cases appeals in civil proceedings may go direct from the High Court to the House of Lords.

One modification of this entirely municipal system of courts is provided by certain articles of the treaties establishing the European Communities, which, since the European Communities Act 1972, now bind the whole of the United Kingdom. Where any question regarding the interpretation of the European treaties, or regarding the interpretation or validity of the acts of the institutions of the Communities, is raised before a court or tribunal of any member state, that court or tribunal may request the *European Court of Justice* to give a ruling thereon before proceeding further with the case in hand. And such a reference to the European Court must be made if there is no further judicial remedy against the ultimate decision of the court or tribunal concerned. Accordingly there will be some circumstances in which the House of Lords, and any other court or tribunal which is of last resort, will be bound first to refer questions to the European Court. The judges of the Court of

Justice are drawn from the member states, there being one from each state, plus one other.

At this stage the *Judicial Committee of the Privy Council* should also be mentioned, as it is the ultimate court of appeal from the courts of the Isle of Man, the Channel Islands, the various colonies and dependencies of the United Kingdom, and from the courts of such of the independent members of the Commonwealth as have not abolished the right of appeal to it.[8] The Committee also hears certain appeals from special tribunals, such as the General Medical Council, and gives advice to Parliament upon legal matters which may occasionally be referred to it.[9] The composition of the Board, as it is called, is often the same as for the hearing of appeals in the House of Lords, although Privy Councillors who are not Lords of Appeal are sometimes admitted to membership in view of their judicial experience in other Commonwealth countries. In recent years the membership of the Judicial Committee has been widened, and more Commonwealth judges have been appointed as Privy Councillors so that they might sit for the hearing of appeals. As has been pointed out in Chapter 3, all Lords of Appeal are Privy Councillors. The decisions of the Board are strictly speaking in the form of advice to the Crown, and only one 'judgment' used to be given by the whole Board, but since 1966 it has been permissible for members to deliver dissenting opinions.

B. CRIMINAL COURTS[10]

As before, the *magistrates' courts* are lowest in the hierarchy of courts, but they are of far more importance for the trial of persons charged with criminal offences than in civil proceedings, since they are responsible for the trial summarily of more than 95% of all accused persons. Such trial is of the persons accused of what may be generally described as the less serious offences. Because of the preponderance of this type of crime, particularly in large urban areas, stipendiary magistrates are sometimes appointed to relieve or take the place of JPs, and metropolitan

---

8   Many independent countries have now abolished this right of appeal.
9   See eg *Re Parliamentary Privilege Act 1770* [1958] AC 331, [1958] 2 All ER 329.
10   It is not proposed to discuss the *coroners' courts* here, as they do not actually have the function of trying a case to reach a decision upon any particular person's guilt.

stipendiary magistrates sit in the London boroughs. Specially qualified magistrates sit in *Juvenile Courts* with special powers. Although normally JPs sit as a bench of at least two, a stipendiary or metropolitan stipendiary magistrate may sit alone and have the same powers as any two JPs. Appeals from magistrates' courts in criminal cases lie, as in civil cases, to the *Crown Court* and the *Divisional Court of the Queen's Bench Division*. Any magistrate sitting alone also has the power to examine a person who is accused of a more serious crime, for he must decide whether there is a prima facie case to be answered at a trial with a jury before that person may be committed for trial. Only a magistrate may thus commit a person for trial for an 'indictable' offence.

The trial of all criminal offences of the graver variety is always before a jury, and held in the *Crown Court*. These courts, created by the Courts Act 1971, are held in various centres throughout the country, and they are presided over by High Court Judges, Circuit Judges or Recorders, the latter being barristers or solicitors appointed to act in this judicial capacity on a part-time basis. There is also provision for JPs to sit with a judge when the Crown Court is hearing appeals from the decisions of magistrates' courts. The Crown Court in London retains the name of its predecessor, the *Central Criminal Court*. Appeal from any conviction before a Crown Court lies, at the instance of the defendant only, to the *Criminal Division of the Court of Appeal*, which in any sitting consists normally of two, or occasionally three, judges, one of whom is usually a Lord Justice of Appeal and the other either the Lord Chief Justice or a puisne Judge of the Queen's Bench Division. The *Courts-Martial Appeal Court*, composed in the same way as the criminal division of the Court of Appeal, and first set up by statute in 1951, hears appeals from conviction by courts-martial, but it is not necessary here to consider the disciplinary powers of courts within the armed forces.

Once more the final court of appeal is the *House of Lords*. An appeal lies, at the instance of either the defendant or the prosecutor, from a decision of the criminal division of the Court of Appeal, the Courts-Martial Appeal Court or the Divisional Court wherever the court below certifies that a point of law of general public importance is involved, and it appears either to that court or to the House of Lords that the point is one which ought to be considered by the House.[11] But, in distinction from its civil jurisdiction, the House has no power to hear a criminal appeal from Scotland. The *Judicial Committee of the Privy Council* hears criminal appeals from jurisdictions outside the United Kingdom, but only where it appears that there may have been grave mismanagement or a serious miscarriage of justice.

III. The Doctrine of Precedent

The doctrine of stare decisis, which has been built up in England, and which is mirrored in Scotland and Northern Ireland, provides that decisions of the *House of Lords* are binding upon all lower courts and also usually upon itself. But in 1966 the Lord Chancellor, with the agreement of all the Law Lords, stated that the House of Lords would in future consider itself able to depart from any previous decision of the House when it appears right to do so. Subject to the overriding jurisdiction of the Lords, decisions of the *Court of Appeal* and of the *Divisional Court* are normally binding upon themselves and upon lower courts, but the qualifications upon this statement are too technical to explain in this book.[12] Decisions of the *High Court* or *Crown Court* are probably binding on inferior courts, but they are only highly persuasive upon later sittings of their own courts. All the courts that have been mentioned are regarded as 'superior courts', except for the magistrates' courts and County Courts, which are 'inferior courts'. Decisions of inferior courts do not bind other inferior courts, and they cannot even be regarded as highly persuasive. Any persuasive value which they possess at all is likely to be short-lived, as cases before these courts are not reported in any recognised series of reports.

The precedent value of any court decision is, of course, always subject to alteration by Act of Parliament.

IV. Judicial Tenure

Judges of inferior courts may be removed from office by the Lord Chancellor (though this is a rare occurrence), but Circuit Judges

---

11   Administration of Justice Act 1960 and Criminal Appeal Act 1968.
12   See *Young v Bristol Aeroplane Co* [1944] KB 718, [1944] 2 All ER 293.

may only be so removed on the grounds of incapacity or misbehaviour. It is of particular importance, however, that all judges of superior courts (that is, High Court Judges and above) have a much greater safeguard to their tenure of office. Although they must retire at the age of 75, they may in practice only be removed before that age by the Crown after an address requesting such removal by both Houses of Parliament. This provision was first enacted in the Act of Settlement 1701, and the relevant statutes in force today are the Surpreme Court Act 1981 and the Appellate Jurisdiction Act 1876 (concerning Lords of Appeal in Ordinary).[13] Although it is sometimes alleged that it is undesirable that the judiciary should depend for their continued tenure of office upon the goodwill of the legislature, it is significant that over a period of 285 years no English judges have ever been so removed.[14] In addition the salary of all judges is charged on the Consolidated Fund, and is not reviewed each year by the House of Commons with the other estimates of national expenditure.

There is, however, a possible restriction upon the tenure of the higher judiciary which was introduced by the Supreme Court Act 1981. If the Lord Chancellor is satisfied, by means of a medical certificate, that any judge of the Supreme Court is disabled by permanent infirmity from performing his judicial duties, and is for the time being incapacitated from resigning his office, he may declare that judge's office to have been vacated. In the case of the Lord Chief Justice, the Master of the Rolls, the President of the Family Division or the Vice-Chancellor, the declaration requires the concurrence of two of their number; in the case of a Lord Justice of Appeal it requires the concurrence of the Master of the Rolls; and in the case of a puisne Judge of any Division of the High Court it requires the concurrence of the senior judge of that Division. Although no judge's office has yet been declared vacant under this procedure, it is surely reasonable to have this power available in the event of, eg, a judge being rendered paralysed and speechless by a stroke. This modification of the principle of judicial independence established by the Act of Settlement is thus no significant infringement of judicial tenure.

13 A possible reserve power to dismiss, vested in the Crown alone, is discussed in eg, Hood Phillips, *Constitutional and Administrative Law* (6th edn, 1978) p 383.
14 It is, however, fair to add that some danger may exist where the British model concerning judicial tenure is copied in Commonwealth countries, where sometimes the political system is not yet as stable as in the United Kingdom.

FURTHER READING

H. G. Hanbury and D. C. M. Yardley *English Courts of Law* (5th edn, by D. C. M. Yardley 1979)

G. R. Y. Radcliffe and Lord Cross of Chelsea *The English Legal System* (6th edn, by G. J. Hand and D. J. Bentley, 1977)

A. K. R. Kiralfy *The English Legal System* (6th edn, 1978)

O. Hood Phillips and A. H. Hudson *A First Book of English Law* (7th edn, 1977)

R. M. Jackson *The Machinery of Justice in England* (7th edn, 1977)

R. J. Walker and M. G. Walker *The English Legal System* (5th edn, 1980)

K. J. Eddey *The English Legal System* (3rd edn, 1982)

Chapter 5

The Rule of Law

Few phrases in recent years have become so well known by all members of the community as 'the rule of law', and yet it is doubtful whether many of the people who commonly use the expression have more than a very vague idea what they mean by it. It is used most frequently by politicians and statesmen who essay to decry the actions of other political parties or foreign governments on the ground that they do not measure up to the standards of common decency and fair dealing which they themselves believe they stand for. This use of the term is not incorrect, for it is not a technical expression, but it is certainly not a use which stems from any exact knowledge of its meaning; and as lawyers it is important that we should be able to define as far as possible the type of fair dealing to be regarded as the standard behaviour within the meaning of the expression. The most logical attempt in the sphere of international affairs that has been made to discover and explain the meaning of the phrase has been by the International Commission of Jurists, an independent international organisation, not set up by the United Nations, but enjoying consultative status with the United Nations Economic and Social Council. The purpose of the International Commission is to draw the attention of all governments and peoples to any actions by any country or government anywhere in the world which have the effect of curtailing the basic liberties of any members of the community.[1]

The activities of statesmen, and even of lawyers, in the international sphere are not, however, of any immediate significance in municipal British constitutional law. Yet the rule of law is still of some importance within that municipal law, and it is therefore our duty to investigate its nature and function. In doing so we must to some extent anticipate the contents of Part

1 Such basic liberties in the United Kingdom are discussed in Chapter 8, below.

II of this book, for many developments in English administrative law have provided useful illustrations of the working of the rule of law. But it is best to leave consideration of the scope and details of administrative law until the basic principles of constitutional law have been explained. Many jurists through the centuries have been interested in the concept of the rule of law, but any modern discussion of the subject must begin with the theory of Professor A. V. Dicey, first published in 1885 in his *Introduction to the Study of the Law of the Constitution*, because discussion of the concept in this country has for the past ninety years centred round his ideas about the expression. Dicey divided the rule of law into three parts, explained by the following extracts:

> 1 '. . . no man is punishable or can be lawfully made to suffer in body or goods except for a distinct breach of law established in the ordinary legal manner before the ordinary Courts of the land. In this sense the rule of law is contrasted with every system of government based on the exercise by persons in authority of wide, arbitrary, or discretionary powers of constraint . . . It means, in the first place, the absolute supremacy or predominance of regular law as opposed to the influence of arbitrary power, and excludes the existence of arbitrariness, of prerogative or even a wide discretionary authority on the part of the government.'[2]
>
> 2 '. . . every man, whatever be his rank or condition, is subject to the ordinary law of the realm and amenable to the jurisdiction of the ordinary tribunals.'[3]
>
> 3 '. . . the general principles of the constitution (as for example the right to personal liberty or the right of public meeting) are with us the result of judicial decisions determining the rights of private persons in particular cases brought before the Courts; whereas under many foreign constitutions the security (such as it is) given to the rights of individuals results, or appears to result, from the general principles of the constitution . . . Our constitution, in short, is a judge-made constitution . . .'[4]

It can be seen that the first two parts of the rule are closely allied,

---

2   Op cit, (10th edn, 1959) pp 188, 202.
3   Op cit, p 193.
4   Op cit, pp 195, 196.

and may be said to amount to the concept of equality before the law for all citizens. The maxim *nullum crimen sine lege* would be apposite here. It may be noted that the arbitrary rule of the Nazi Government in Germany and elsewhere in the 1930s and 1940s, with the accompanying activities of the Gestapo, was in clear breach of the first part of Dicey's rule, as are also the totalitarian acts of the many Communist governments today. Dicey did in fact go on to contrast English law with that of France, in which country there existed (as there still exists today) a separate system of administrative courts, which had jurisdiction over all disputes between the state and individuals, to the exclusion of the ordinary courts of law. Many critics of Dicey have believed that he was asserting that no such thing as administrative law existed in this country, but such criticism has been unjust, for he intended to say no more than that we had no separate *droit administratif* with its own special courts. As was clear to him and to all English lawyers, there must always be a branch of law amounting to administrative law, because no country can survive without an administration, and any such administration must possess certain legal rights, powers and duties which impinge in some way upon the lives and rights of the ordinary citizens of the land. Dicey did in fact publish a paper in the *Law Quarterly Review* in 1915, entitled 'The Development of Administrative Law in England',[5] and it is now clear that he only intended to declare that in this country the ordinary courts had jurisdiction over questions of administrative law, just as over all branches of the law, whatever the rules of those branches may be. Where he was wrong was in believing that the French system favoured the state to the detriment of the rights of the ordinary citizens of France, and that thus the existence of the administrative courts was in conflict with the rule of law. If one accepts Dicey's distinction between the two systems as correct, with the exception of his mistaken distrust of the French administrative courts, and that the ordinary courts deal with English administrative law problems, then there is one way at least in which the laws of the United Kingdom may have progressed away from the concept of the rule of law since the time of his writing, for, as we shall see in Chapter 11, a large number of administrative tribunals have been created since his time, and these tribunals have jurisdiction over much litigation of all kinds in the field of administrative law. There existence may be strictly contrary to Dicey's first branch of the rule, but at least none of them ought to favour the executive to the derogation of the rights of individuals, and all are subject to control by the ordinary courts of the land, as will be explained in Chapter 11.

It is not hard to find a number of other examples in our laws which must be exceptions to the first two branches of Dicey's concept. Foreign sovereigns and diplomats enjoy special immunity from criminal prosecution or civil action, and judges can never be held civilly liable for anything done or said in the course of their office. Members of both Houses of Parliament enjoy extensive privileges, which have already been discussed in Chapter 2, while peers are disqualified from voting in parliamentary elections. Trades Unions occupy a specially privileged position in that they cannot normally be rendered liable in tort at all,[6] although this legal immunity was only conferred for the first time by the Trades Disputes Act 1906, some 20 years after Dicey first published his theory, and it has been somewhat reduced by provisions in the Employment Act 1982. Police powers of arrest without warrant may be regarded as infringements upon individual liberty, even though they are unlikely to be used in an entirely arbitrary manner in this country.[7] Discretionary powers may always be conferred upon the executive, or indeed upon anyone, by Act of Parliament, the most usual example being the power to make delegated legislation,[8] and powers of a somewhat similar nature may be conferred also by the Royal Prerogative.[9] But at the time of Dicey's writing probably the most glaring exception from his rule was the immunity from the ordinary process of law which had been accorded to the Crown as a result of the royal prerogative, an immunity in which Parliament had acquiesced, for it could be useful to the government or to any future government. As we shall see in Chapter 11, this exception has been largely eliminated by the passage of the Crown Proceedings

---

6   For a powerful condemnation of the present Trade Union immunity, see Lord MacDermott *Protection from Power under English Law* (1957) Ch 7; and see the Trade Union and Labour Relations Act 1974.
7   See Chapter 8, below.
8   See Chapter 10, below.
9   See Chapter 10, below.

Act 1947 and it is now true to say that in one very important respect our law has approached more nearly to the concept of the rule of law which Dicey had propounded.

It would be impossible to iron out all the inequalities. Perhaps the most clear example of all inequalities which are essential in civilised communities is provided by the age of criminal responsibility. It is unthinkable that a new-born baby or a very young child should bear full criminal responsibility for his activities. So the rule of law, even for Dicey, cannot have meant equal *treatment* for all before the law. It is enough that the same law covers us all, even though it makes different provisions for different groups of people—and it is of course always possible for the ordinary citizen to join a Trade Union or to become an MP. Yet the fact that the various exceptions within the law may be recognised by the law in a totalitarian state is not enough to satisfy the principle of the rule of law. As the International Commission of Jurists has repeatedly stressed, a legal system must also provide for a proper balance, with judicial safeguards, between the interests of the state and of individuals, an independent judiciary and Bar, and social institutions allowing for the dignity of man.

The third branch of Dicey's rule is largely true, provided it is accepted that the concept of the sovereignty of Parliament is based on the decisions of the courts to that effect. Certainly it is true that the constitution is part of the ordinary law of the land, and is not contained in any special instrument or instruments. The sovereignty of Parliament has been discussed already in Chapter 2, and we need not elaborate upon it further here, but its very existence renders the first two branches of Dicey's rule subject to a possible enormous practical exception.

The great value of Dicey's work in this field has been to provide lawyers and jurists with an ideal. It is not possible to formulate a satisfactory definition of the rule of law, and indeed it cannot seriously be contended that any one 'rule' as such has any place in the law of the United Kingdom, which depends primarily on the rules laid down by Parliament and secondarily upon the concrete decisions of the courts. If such a theoretical 'rule' has no place among the detailed statutes and decisions from which our law is drawn, then it cannot be considered as a basic tenet of our constitutional law. But as a guide to law-makers and reformers it can be of inestimable value, and for this purpose it is of little importance whether one accepts the views of Dicey or of any other jurist,[10] or constructs an entirely new idea concerning its identity. Providing the aim is the preservation of the liberty and rights of all members of the community, and that only such exceptions from this aim are allowed as are essential to the administration of the nation in an orderly fashion (such as judicial and parliamentary privilege, with proper safeguards), the purpose of the rule of law will have been fulfilled. In short, the rule of law is not a rule or a law, but a persuasive guide for the legislature, the executive and the judiciary, linked in practice, in the United Kingdom, with the working of many of the conventions which mitigate the theoretical deficiencies in the Constitution, and mould it into a living democratic entity.

FURTHER READING

A. V. Dicey *Introduction to the Study of the Law of the Constitution* (10th edn, by E. C. S. Wade, 1959)
Sir W. Ivor Jennings *The Law and the Constitution* (5th edn, 1959)
The various publications of the International Commission of Jurists.

---

10 See eg, E. C. S. Wade and G. Godfrey Phillips *Constitutional and Administrative Law* (9th edn) Ch 6.

Chapter 6

The Doctrine of the Separation of Powers

It is submitted that the three basic and essential functions in the administration of any independent state are legislative, executive and judicial. From a realisation of this generally accepted opinion has sprung at various times and in different countries the idea that the agencies through which these functions are exercised should be kept separate from each other, the intention being to prevent the concentration of more than one of the powers in any single authority, which might lead to tyranny, and to make sure that the due exercise of each is in no way hindered by the agencies responsible for the other two. Theories concerning the best methods of carrying out this intention go back as far as Aristotle, and find expression in the constitutions of many nations, although in no country is the doctrine practised in such a way as to render the three functions entirely exclusive.

The Constitution of the United States of America, which came into effect on 4 March 1789, probably provides us with the most extreme example of a practical separation of the three fundamental powers.[1] It is based upon a mistaken interpretation by the French writer Montesquieu of the position in England in the eighteenth century,[2] though it should be added that the founding fathers were interested in Montesquieu's views as applied to America, and they were in no way concerned about whether or not he had interpreted the English Constitution of his time accurately. The first three articles of the United States Constitution vest federal legislative powers in Congress, the executive power in the President, and the judicial power in the

---

1 The Constitution of the State of Massachusetts may possibly be more extreme in some respects.
2 *De l'Esprit des Lois*, Ch VI, paras 3–6. In fact, as Madison pointed out in *The Federalist*, Montesquieu was mainly concerned to warn against the dangers of monopoly of power, and he may therefore have been less mistaken than is sometimes asserted.

75

Supreme Court of the United States. These powers appear to have been intended for the most part to be mutually exclusive, so that no member of one branch of government may be a member of either of the others as well, but even so the separation was not complete, and various 'checks and balances' between the three agencies were provided. Thus, the President is empowered to veto legislation of Congress, and such a veto may be overrriden by a two-thirds majority in each House of Congress. Any treaties which the President enters into with other countries must be ratified by a two-thirds majority in the Senate before they may come into effect. Although the normal rule is that no member of the government may also be a member of Congress, yet the Vice-President ex officio presides over the Senate. The President appoints judges to office in the Supreme Court, and finally, even though there is no provision for this in the Constitution itself, it has been found essential that the Supreme Court should have the power to declare Acts of Congress (or of any state legislature) or actions of the President illegal if they should in any way transgress the provisions of the federal Constitution.[3] The system in the United States has justly been described as a separation of powers modified by checks and balances.

Turning to the United Kingdom, it is clear that the three fundamental powers exist, just as they exist in other countries, and they have been described in Chapters 2, 3 and 4 of this book. The legislative power is vested in Parliament, the executive power in the Crown, and the judicial power in the courts of law. In the earlier chapters we have endeavoured to point out both the existence of these basic functions and also their essential differences in nature, but it has become apparent that there is much overlapping between them and between the authorities in which the powers are vested. This is therefore the place at which to summarise the principal factors which in the United Kingdom render it impossible to insist that any strict separation of powers exists. As in the last chapter, it will be necessary in part to refer forward to certain material included in the later chapters of the book, but it is thought best to provide a complete picture of the position at this earlier stage.

(1) Members of the government are usually members of one or

---

3   For a short but stimulating discussion of this topic, see Learned Hand *The Bill of Rights* (1958). See also Chapter 4, above.

other of the Houses of Parliament, because it is desirable that all ministers of the Crown should be held responsible to Parliament for their actions.[4] This is not an absolute rule, as may be seen from the case of Sir Frank Soskice, who was defeated in his constituency at the 1950 general election, but nevertheless retained his ministerial position as Attorney-General, being elected to the Commons in a by-election when another member of the Labour Party stood down from his own seat; or of Mr Gordon Walker, who became Foreign Secretary in the Labour Government which came to power in 1964, despite his own defeat at the general election of that year, and who only resigned that office after his defeat at a later by-election. Probably a member of the government may retain his office providing he does not cease to be a member of one of the Houses of Parliament for more than a few months. It is, however, more usual for any minister who takes office without possessing a seat in either House to be created a peer so that he may sit in the Lords. It may be noted that one of the most useful methods of checking up on the activities of ministers or of the government as a whole is the parliamentary question: there is no such parallel possibility in the United States, where members of the government do not sit in Congress, and there is no 'question time'. The concept of ministerial responsibility to Parliament has been copied in the constitutions of most independent Commonwealth countries.[5]

(2) The monarch, who heads the government, also in effect forms the 'third House of Parliament'.[6] Both this point and the last one lead to the common usage of 'Parliament' and 'government' as interchangeable terms, although such a practice is of course incorrect. It will be recalled that the government, through its parliamentary majority, holds the whip-hand in the House of Commons, and thus can usually force legislation through that House, and ultimately through Parliament as a whole.[7]

(3) The monarch is the 'fountain of justice', being technically present in all his courts of law, responsible for many judicial appointments, and exercising the prerogative of mercy in respect of persons convicted in the courts.[8] Thus he plays a part in all three of the fundamental powers.

---

4 See Chapters 2 and 3, above.
5 See Chapter 13, below.
6 See Chapter 2, above.
7 See Chapters 2 and 3, above.
8 See Chapters 3 and 4, above.

(4) Parliament is strictly called the 'High Court of Parliament', and although the House of Commons carries out no judicial functions today, the House of Lords is still the ultimate court of appeal.[9] The Lords of Appeal in Ordinary sit in the House of Lords both as a legislative body and as a court, and they are also Privy Councillors, as is indeed the Speaker of the House of Commons.[10] The Lord Chancellor also plays a part in all three of the powers, being a member of the House of Lords as a legislative body and as a court, responsible for a number of judicial appointments, and also a member of the government.

(5) Although the independence of the judiciary is in practice jealously preserved,[11] superior judges are appointed by the Crown or by the Lord Chancellor, and are removable by the Crown on an address by both Houses of Parliament to the Crown, while inferior judges are appointed and removable by the Lord Chancellor.[12]

(6) The power to make delegated legislation is usually vested by Act of Parliament in the government.[13]

(7) Administrative tribunals, as well as many of the ordinary courts of law,[14] are created either directly by Act of Parliament or by delegated powers conferred upon ministers by statute. Their powers and duties may be both judicial and administrative.[15]

(8) Justices of the Peace are primarily judges, but still retain certain administrative duties, such as licensing.[16]

(9) Local government powers are created by Parliament or by Royal Charter and are both legislative and executive within the district of each local authority.[17]

Enough has been said to show the interrelation between the three fundamental powers. It is very probable that the overlapping of powers and authorities insures against arbitrariness. It may be added, finally, that the all-powerful position of Parliament makes it possible for the legislature to make any

---

9   See Chapters 2 and 4, above.
10   See Chapters 2, 3 and 4, above.
11   See Chapter 4, above.
12   See Chapters 3 and 4, above.
13   See Chapter 10, below.
14   See Chapter 4, above.
15   See Chapter 11, below.
16   See Chapter 4, above.
17   See Chapter 12, below.

alteration in the present system which it may wish by simple Act of Parliament. This is not only the method of passing ordinary legislation in the United Kingdom, but it is the procedure for effecting any constitutional amendment whatever.[18]

FURTHER READING

C. S. Emden *Principles of British Constitutional Law* (1925)
B. Schwartz *American Constitutional Law* (1955)

---

18 See Chapter 2, above.

Chapter 7

Scotland, Wales, Northern Ireland, the Isle of Man and the Channel Islands

In the present chapter it is intended briefly to sketch the importance so far as British constitutional law is concerned of those other parts of the British Isles which are not automatically subject to the municipal law of England. The relationships between each of these countries have already been mentioned in Chapter 1.

I. Scotland and Wales

The separate Kingdoms of England and Scotland became associated by the personal union of the Crowns of both countries when James VI of Scotland succeeded to the throne of England as King James I in 1603, but the complete unification of the two countries in a political sense did not occur until the Treaty of Union, which was ratified by Acts of the two Parliaments of England and Scotland in 1707. The effect of the Treaty and Acts was to abolish the two Parliaments and to form a new Parliament of Great Britain, and thus ultimately a government of the whole country, in Westminster. This position has been altered by the later union with Ireland, discussed below, only to the extent of increasing the jurisdiction of Parliament to cover the whole of the newly formed United Kingdom, and the full legislative authority of Parliament over both countries remains.[1] It has, however, remained customary to appoint six or seven members of each government to special responsibility over Scottish affairs, and in particular there is always a Secretary of State for Scotland.

The Scottish courts of law, legal professions and legal systems

---

1 With the possible exception exemplified in the case of *MacCormick v Lord Advocate* 1953 SC 396, discussed in Chapter 2, above.

have not been affected by the union, except in so far as Parliamentary authority was transferred to Westminister, and that the House of Lords became the ultimate court of appeal, though only in civil cases, as has been seen above in Chapter 4. The legal systems of England and Scotland have had widely different histories and traditions, but it is not our present purpose to examine them. The superior Scottish civil courts are the Inner and Outer Houses of the Court of Session, of which the Inner House, which sits in two Divisions, presided over by the Lord President and the Lord Justice-Clerk respectively, exercises appellate jurisdiction, while ten Lords of Session sit singly in the Outer House, as Lords Ordinary, to hear cases at first instance. The superior criminal court is the High Court of Justiciary, consisting of the same judges as the Court of Session but under the titles of Lord Justice-General, Lord Justice-Clerk and Lords Commissioners of Justiciary, which exercises both trial jurisdiction (one Lord with a jury) in Edinburgh or on circuit, and appellate jurisdiction. The inferior courts in criminal cases are the district courts, and in civil matters the Sheriff Courts, presided over by Sheriffs. Appeals lie in civil cases either to the Sheriff Principal and then on to the Inner House of the Court of Session, or directly to the Inner House of the Court of Session, and in criminal cases to the High Court of Justiciary. The Scottish equivalent of the English Attorney-General is the Lord Advocate, though he does not occupy the position of head of the Scottish Bar.

In recent years there has been a movement in favour of some devolution of legislative and executive power from Westminster to Scotland and Wales. The Report of the Royal Commission on the Constitution, published in 1973,[2] recommended the establishment of separate Scottish and Welsh Assemblies, though the Commissioners were unable to agree on many of the details of their proposals. The recommendations were in any case highly contentious and politically charged, but the Labour Government, after first publishing a White Paper detailing its intentions, introduced a Scotland and Wales Bill into Parliament. The main purpose of the Bill was to establish an Assembly and an Executive in Scotland, which should have legislative and executive powers over a fairly wide range of topics, and a smaller

[2] Cmnd 5460.

Assembly in Wales, with only executive powers and over a rather more limited range of topics. Powers of veto were to be retained by the Secretaries of State for Scotland and Wales respectively, and the whole of the power to tax should remain at Westminster. The Bill attracted opposition in the House of Commons not only from the Conservative Opposition but also from a number of Labour dissidents and some of the smaller parties, and it had to be abandoned after the government was defeated on a timetable motion in February 1977.

Towards the end of the same year the government then introduced two Bills designed to achieve devolution of some power to the two provinces separately, and this time it was successful in steering them through Parliament. The Scotland Act 1978 and the Wales Act 1978 duly received the royal assent, but each Act provided that it should only come into opeation on such day as the Secretary of State should by order appoint, and that any such order required the approval by resolution of both Houses of Parliament. But no draft of such an order was to be laid before Parliament until a referendum had been held in the province concerned. A referendum was then held in Scotland and in Wales in March 1979, when the question asked was: 'Do you want the provisions of the Scotland (or Wales) Act, 1978, to be put into effect?' If it appeared to the Secretary of State, having regard to the answers in the referendum and all other circumstances, that the Act should not be brought into effect, he was then empowered to lay before Parliament a draft Order-in-Council providing for its repeal, and this draft would require to be approved by Parliament in the same way as an order to bring the Act into force. In the event the results of the referenda showed a majority in favour of the proposed devolution in Scotland which was insufficient to justify bringing the provisions of the Scotland Act into force, and a 4–1 majority against such devolution in Wales. Accordingly one of the first acts of the Conservative Government which came to power after the General Election of May 1979 was to obtain the approval of Parliament for the repeal of the two Acts by Order-in-Council. Nevertheless it remains a possibility that some further scheme for devolution of power to Scotland or Wales, may emerge at a future date.

II. Northern Ireland

Northern Ireland is a part of the United Kingdom of Great Britain and Northern Ireland, as has already be seen in Chapter 1. Its law, like that of England and Wales, is a common law system, in that it is derived partly from parliamentary statutes and partly from case law decided in the courts of the land. Prior to the Act of Union with Ireland in 1800, the Parliament of Ireland had legislative authority over the whole of Ireland, although some authority was at times claimed by the Parliament of England (up till 1707) and by the Parliament of Great Britain (between 1707 and 1800), for Ireland held the status of a lesser Kingdom under the English, and later the British, Crown. Between 1800 and 1922 only the Parliament of the United Kingdom of Great Britain and Ireland had this authority; and after the Irish Free State (Agreement) Act 1922, which followed the partition of Northern and Southern Ireland (the latter having since become the Republic of Ireland, and separate from the British Crown), the legislative power over Northern Ireland was held partly by the United Kingdom Parliament in Westminster and partly by the Northern Ireland Parliament at Stormont.

The Constitution of Northern Ireland, as laid down in the Government of Ireland Act 1920, involving the partition of Ireland and the creation of the Stormont Parliament, was always a matter of contention and gave rise from time to time to extremist action of a violent nature. As a result of a particularly serious wave of disorder and terrorism starting in 1969, the British Parliament prorogued the Stormont Parliament by the Northern Ireland (Temporary Provisions) Act 1972, and imposed direct rule over the province from Westminster, such rule being exercised by a new Secretary of State for Northern Ireland. The government made it clear at the time that it was intended as soon as possible to make further provisions for devolution of power to the province, and such provisions were made in the Northern Ireland Assembly Act 1973, and the Northern Ireland Constitution Act 1973, which also includes a charter of human rights for the province. In view of the fact that the Unionist Party had been in the majority in Stormont continuously from 1922 to 1972, and that no other party had been able to take part in the formation of the Northern Ireland Executive, it was provided that elections to the new Assembly were to be by a type of proportional representation, so that the proportion of members of the various political parties in the Assembly would largely mirror the number of votes cast for the parties at the preceding election for the Assembly. The Executive also, when formed, was to consist of members of both the majority and minority groups. The Act did not stipulate how the mixed Executive was to be set up, but appointments were to be made by the Secretary of State for Northern Ireland, who was to be satisfied that the Executive was likely to be widely accepted throughout the community.

Unfortunately both the Assembly and the new Executive proved to be unworkable because the different political parties refused to work with each other. The Assembly, although elected only in 1973, was therefore dissolved, along with the Executive, less than a year later by the Northern Ireland Act 1974. The 1974 Act also made provision for a Constitutional Convention, which was elected in 1975. Its function was to work out a means of forming a power-sharing administration for Northern Ireland. But again the new body failed, this time because the United Ulster Unionists, who had an overall majority of members of the Convention refused to make any recommendation for power-sharing with other parties. Eventually the Convention was dissolved in 1976, and direct rule over the province from Westminster reimposed.

The latest attempt to devolve power to Northern Ireland is the Northern Ireland Act 1982, which makes arrangements for what has been called 'rolling devolution'. Under the Act there is provision for election to a new Northern Ireland Assembly, which will at first possess only scrutinising, deliberative and consultative functions. The first election to this Assembly took place in October 1982 by the single transferable voting system. The Assembly is asked to recommend to the Secretary of State arrangements under which the whole or part of the range of legislative and executive responsibilities previously transferred by the 1973 legislation could be exercised by the Assembly and by a devolved administration answerable to it. Then, provided certain criteria are satisfied, the Government will recommend to Parliament that the arrangements so recommended should be implemented and appropriate powers transferred.

The above legislation left untouched the arrangements

whereby twelve MPs are elected in Northern Ireland constituencies for the House of Commons at Westminster, where they possess equal powers and status with members elected from other parts of the Kingdom. But the House of Commons (Redistribution of Seats) Act 1979 makes provision for the number of Northern Ireland seats in the Commons to be increased to between 16 and 18, the exact number to be settled after a report from the Northern Ireland Boundary Commission. The eventual result has been to increase the number of seats to 17.

The law of Northern Ireland, although strictly an entirely separate system from that of England, is in practice very like it, partly because of the long history of close association, and later actual union, with the mother country, and partly because its legal development today tends to mirror that of its British partner. The courts of Northern Ireland are very like those of England. Thus there is a Supreme Court of Judicature of Northern Ireland, consisting of a Crown Court, a High Court and a Court of Appeal, the latter of which sits in Belfast. Further appeals from the Court of Appeal in civil cases, and in criminal cases under similar conditions to those which exist in England, lie to the House of Lords at Westminster, which in such cases must act as the highest court of appeal for purposes of Northern Ireland law. The officers and judges of the Northern Ireland courts bear similar titles to those of their English counterparts.

III. The Isle of Man

The Isle of Man is a separate dependency of the British Crown, and is not part of the United Kingdom, although Acts of the United Kingdom Parliament will apply to the island provided they do so expressly or by necessary implication. The legislature, one of the oldest in the world, is called the Court of Tynwald, and it is composed of the Lieutenant-Governor, the Legislative Council and the House of Keys. Until 1980 the Lieutenant-Governor presided over the Legislative Council, the other members being the Bishop of Sodor and Man, the First Deemster, the Attorney-General, and seven members elected by the House of Keys. However the Legislative Council now has its own separate elected president, and the other former ex officio members of the Council have since been excluded from it. The

House of Keys consists of 24 elected members, and there must be a fresh election at least every five years. The Tynwald is responsible for most internal legislation, which must receive the royal assent, but certain important subjects, such as air navigation and merchant shipping, are usually dealt with by the United Kingdom Parliament.

The executive authority is vested in the Lieutenant-Governor, who is responsible, among other things, for defence, but in recent years he has been assisted by an Executive Council, over which he has, since 1980, ceased to preside. The royal assent to legislation of the Tynwald is normally signified through the Lieutenant-Governor.

The law of the island, known as 'breast law', is quite distinct from English law, though it tends more and more to resemble the latter today. The courts of the island are also distinct, and the judges are called Deemsters. The most important courts are the Staff of Government, which deals with civil cases, and the Court of Criminal Appeal, from either of which a further appeal lies to the Judicial Committee of the Privy Council.

IV. The Channel Islands

The Channel Islands may in a sense claim to have been older dependencies of the English Crown than any other parts of the present British Isles, for they belonged to the Dukes of Normandy before England was annexed to the Duchy. The two main islands are Jersey and Guernsey, Alderney and Sark being dependencies of the latter. Although the islanders in theory deny the right of the United Kingdom Parliament to legislate for them, in practice they do not dispute it, and United Kingdom legislation is frequently extended to the islands by Order in Council. The laws of the islands are of Norman origin, and are distinct from those of England. A word or two should be said about each island:

(1) JERSEY   •

The local legislature is the States of Jersey, consisting of the Bailiff, who is nominated by the Crown and who presides, the Attorney-General, Solicitor-General, the Dean of Jersey, 12 senators, who are elected for 9 years, 12 constables or mayors of the parishes and 28 deputies, who are elected for 3 years. The royal assent is necessary before any legislation may come into force. The Lieutenant-Governor and certain island officials hold executive authority, and the Royal Court, presided over by the Bailiff or Deputy Bailiff, hears both civil and criminal cases, there being an appeal to the Court of Appeal for the Channel Islands, and a further appeal to the Privy Council in civil cases and also, with special leave of the Privy Council, in criminal cases where there may have been a grave miscarriage of justice.

(2) GUERNSEY

The institutions of the Bailiwick of Guernsey are mainly similar to those of Jersey. The States, however, consists of the Bailiff, Attorney-General, Solicitor-General, 12 conseillers, 33 elected People's Deputies and 12 elected douzeniers. *Alderney*, although a dependency, maintains its own legislature, consisting of a President and 9 members, all elected. *Sark*, another dependency, remains a feudal seignory, under the titular control of the hereditary Seigneur or Dame of Sark. Its legislature is the Chief Pleas, consisting of the Seigneur, the Seneschal, who is appointed by the Seigneur with the approval of the Lieutenant-Governor of Guernsey, 12 elected deputies and the 40 tenement holders.

FURTHER READING

G. W. Keeton and D. Lloyd, with specialist contributors *The United Kingdom, The Development of its Laws and Constitutions: Part I. England and Wales, Northern Ireland and the Isle of Man* (1955)

T. B. Smith and L. A. Sheridan *The United Kingdom, The Development of its Laws and Constitutions: Part II. Scotland and the Channel Islands* (1955) (replaced, so far as Scotland only is concerned, by Professor Smith's later book: see below)

T. B. Smith *Scotland: The Development of its Laws and Constitution* (1962) (also published in Scotland as *A Short Commentary on the Law of Scotland*)

H. Calvert *Constitutional Law in Northern Ireland* (1968)

D. M. Walker *The Scottish Legal System* (5th edn, 1981)

Chapter 8

Rights and Duties of the Citizen

In many written constitutions the fundamental rights of the citizen are specifically set out in the constitutional document, as in the first eight and the fourteenth amendments to the Constitution of the United States of America, or, to take a modern example, in the earlier articles of the Constitution of India, which came into force in January 1950. But of course this is not the case as regards the inhabitants of the United Kingdom, for we have no such constitutional document. It would, however, be unrealistic to consider that the citizens of a democratic state should possess no guarantees safeguarding their individual liberties, for such could only result from a recognition that the state was itself of a totalitarian rather than a democratic nature. Similarly it would be unrealistic to consider that the same citizens were under no corresponding duties to their fellow-citizens and to the nation as a whole. Nevertheless it is as well to remember that such individual rights and duties as do exist in the United Kingdom are always subject to the overall power of alteration or abolition by Act of Parliament, for, as we have already seen in Chapter 2, the most basic of all constitutional factors in the United Kingdom is the unrestricted legislative power of Parliament.

In recent years there has been some pressure of a political nature for the enactment of formal statutory civil rights for the United Kingdom. It is not without interest that in the Northern Ireland Constitution Act 1973 there is for the first time a charter of human rights for the province, and that in particular it lays down that any legislation or executive action which is discriminatory on political or religious grounds is unlawful. Perhaps this could be a forerunner of similar legislation for the United Kingdom as a whole, or at least for any action taken in Scotland or Wales if power is ever devolved to those countries from Westminster. It is, however, of note that the Standing

Advisory Commission on Human Rights reported in 1977[1] that, although it favoured the incorporation of the European Convention on Human Rights 1950 into the domestic law of the United Kingdom as a whole, it could see no advantage in enacting more comprehensive civil liberties provisions for Northern Ireland alone. Such legislation of itself can neither cure violence nor create a consensus upon which to base a further effort at devolved government for the province.

1. Rights of the Citizen in the United Kingdom

The declaration of rights of the citizen in the modern sense really dates from the latter part of the eighteenth century, when the revolutions in America and France took place. The theorists and politicians of both these countries borrowed their ideas from the writings of Locke, who, after the Bloodless Revolution of 1688–1689, wrote about natural rights in his *Two Treatises of Civil Government*. Blackstone in the mid-eighteenth century had also lectured and written on the subject of the individual's fundamental rights,[2] and his influence was greatly felt upon the laws and the Constitution of the United States.[3] The American Declaration of Independence in 1776 and the so-called 'Bill of Rights' (the constitutional amendments mentioned above[4]) in 1791 provided inter alia for the preservation of such fundamental rights as freedom of religion, speech, the press, peaceful assembly, and that there should be no deprivation of life, liberty or property without due process of law. The French Declaration of the Rights of Man in 1789 covers very much similar ground, and a far more recent example of such an instrument is provided by the Universal Declaration of Human Rights, adopted by the United Nations General Assembly in 1948, although it may well be felt that the statesmen of some of the countries which supported the latter Declaration did so with their tongues in their cheeks, and certain International Covenants on Human

---

1 *The Protection of Human Rights by Law in Northern Ireland*, Cmnd 7009.
2 *Commentaries on the Laws of England* Vol 1.
3 See H. G. Hanbury *The Vinerian Chair and Legal Education* (1958) Ch III.
4 The first eight amendments apply to federal rights, and the fourteenth amendment applies to the states.

Rights adopted by the General Assembly in 1966. It should be noted that the Universal Declaration of Human Rights has no legal force in any country unless expressly adopted in its municipal law. The same may be said of the European Convention for the Protection of Human Rights and Fundamental Freedoms, drawn up in 1950, though most Western European countries, including the United Kingdom, which subscribed to the Convention, undertook thereby certain basic obligations and agreed to set up, where necessary, machinery for the investigation of an adjudication concerning the civil liberties with which the Convention dealt. The acceptance by the United Kindom government of the competence of the European Commission of Human Rights has already been mentioned in Chapter 2.[5] Its practical effect is that any United Kingdom citizen who has exhausted his domestic legal remedies may apply to the Commission for a remedy against the violation of any of the fundamental rights set out in the European Convention.

In England it is only possible to select certain statutes or charters as having the most significance constitutionally. These purport to perform somewhat similar functions, and include Magna Carta 1215, the Petition of Right 1628, and the Bill of Rights 1689, all having appeared before the time of Locke's writings. None of these documents is really a statute in our modern sense, for they only amount to the acceptance by the monarch of certain demands by Parliament or his people. But they have always been treated as of statutory force. The latter two documents were mainly concerned with the freedom of Parliament in the face of the power of the monarch rather than with the individual liberties of each citizen, and Magna Carta primarily protected the privileges of the barons, but it is the spirit of English law to discover general principles from particular instances.[6] Although there is no need in the present work to examine the documents closely, many basic freedoms have been deduced from them and also from the representative character of Parliament, which, it is argued, would not be permitted by the electorate to exercise such extreme legislative

---

5   Above, p 40.
6   See Roscoe Pound *The Development of Constitutional Guarantees of Liberty* (1957) Chs 1 and 2.

authority unless it did so primarily as a means of protecting and safeguarding the lawful interests and freedoms of the populace. It is therefore assumed that basically all citizens are free to do and act as they please, and that this liberty will only be curtailed in so far as such limitation may be essential for the due and just administration of the whole country, and then only by law and not by arbitrary power. The stability of British institutions, strengthened by the good fortune of centuries of steady growth, unhampered by foreign invasion, is enough to render otiose any more codified list of civil liberties. Even though some prerogative powers cut across individual liberty, they only exist so long as Parliament permits them to remain in the interests of the community, as has already been pointed out in Chapter 3. Thus, as far as British constitutional law is concerned, our main task is to determine in what ways individual liberty is *restricted* by law, and not how it is preserved. We shall also, however, consider the remedies provided by law for the infringement of such funda-mental rights as citizens do possess. Our approach must be primarily negative, but for convenience we may assume that certain basic rights exist except where they have been curtailed by the law, whether statute or common law, and these rights may be said to be:

1 freedom of the person to behave as he pleases,
2 equality before the law,
3 freedom of property,
4 the right to free elections,
5 freedom of speech and to write,
6 freedom of public worship,
7 freedom of assembly and association, and
8 family rights.

It is possible that to this list may be added the right to work and the right to withhold one's labour.

   Some limitations upon the foregoing list are obvious and need not be further explained. Thus freedom of speech and writing must of necessity be restricted by the law of defamation, which in itself is protecting other individuals, and by the laws of sedition, censorship, contempt or court, obscenity, and the prevention of disclosure of official secrets. Freedom of property is subject to the levying of taxes, without which the administration of the country would collapse, and to statutory powers of compulsory acquisition. Again, equality before the law, a concept which has already been discussed in Chapter 5, is a rule with several important exceptions. As has been seen, judges and MPs must receive special protection from ordinary legal process so that they may carry out their duties efficiently, and the same largely applies to diplomats; whereas infants under the age of majority cannot be held fully responsible in law for all their actions.

But other exceptions to the basic freedoms require some explanation. The detailed limitations discussed in this chapter are rules of English law only, unless otherwise indicated, but the laws of Northern Ireland and Scotland are not very dissimilar.

A. *Incursions upon freedom of the person and property*

Every man is free to do as he wishes unless the law otherwise provides, as, for example, by the law of assault, or by the law making it an offence to drive a motor vehicle having consumed alcohol in such a quantity that the proportion in the blood, as ascertained by a compulsory laboratory test, exceeds the prescribed limit.[7] A different statutory limitation may be found in section 3 of the Trades Disputes Act 1906, where it is provided that an act done by a person in contemplation or furtherance of a trade dispute shall not be actionable on the sole ground that it may interfere with the right of some other person to dispose of his capital or his labour as he wills. Thus, by implication, an individual may find his power to dispose of capital or labour hampered without being able to take action to re-establish his right so to dispose of it, unless the person interfering with his right has also offended against the law in some other respect, such as by being guilty of a conspiracy in furtherance of private vengeance.[8] He may of course, as was pointed out in Chapter 5, be powerless to redress the wrong if the additional offence amounts to a tort and it is committed by a Trade Union or Unions, or by Union members in contemplation of furtherance of a trade dispute, as is also provided by the Act of 1906, as subsequently amended.

Any arrest of a person must normally be with the authority of

---

7   A provision first introduced by the Road Safety Act 1967, Pt I.
8   See eg *Huntley v Thornton* [1957] 1 All ER 234, [1957] 1 WLR 321.

a warrant signed by a magistrate and executed by a police officer; and such a warrant will only be issued where the magistrate is satisfied that the grounds for the warrant are lawful. Warrants must name the individual to be arrested specifically, for it was held in 1765[9] that 'general warrants' were illegal. In that case a warrant for the arrest of the authors, printers and publishers of 'The North Briton' was held to be too general. One of the most celebrated of all English constitutional law cases is *Entick v Carrington*, decided in the same year,[10] in which the plaintiff, who was suspected of being the author of 'The Monitor, or British Freeholder', obtained £300 damages for trespass committed by Carrington and certain other King's messengers, who had broken and entered his house and seized his papers and books under a general search warrant issued by a Secretary of State. In petty cases accused persons are 'summoned', and a warrant will only issue if the summons is disobeyed. Arrest without warrant by a police officer is permitted, inter alia, where he has a reasonable suspicion that a person has committed a serious crime, and any other citizen may arrest a person without a warrant where such crime has actually been committed, or if he is called upon to assist a constable or magistrate. There are also certain other special statutory provisions for arrest without warrant which need not concern us here other than to note that they exist. Any person arrested without a warrant must be told, either in technical or non-technical language, the true ground of arrest. It is not sufficient merely to state the general ground, such as 'murder', unless the circumstances are obvious, as when the accused has been caught in the act of committing an offence. In a House of Lords case in 1947[11] two police officers were held liable for false imprisonment after wrongfully arresting the plaintiff without a warrant and misinforming him as to the actual charge to be brought against him.

POLICE POWERS OF SEARCH AND ENTRY

Although the normal rule is that no person may enter private

---

9 *Money v Leach* (1765) 3 Burr 1742.
10 (1765) 19 State Tr 1029.
11 *Christie v Leachinsky* [1947] AC 573, [1947] 1 All ER 567.

premises without permission from the owner or occupant, police may always enter premises to execute a warrant for arrest or to search a person lawfully arrested. It was also held in the famous case of *Elias v Pasmore* in 1934[12] that where police lawfully enter private premises to arrest a man, but do not possess a search warrant, they will still be excused if they take documents or search the premises, provided that they discover something which is useful as evidence in the prosecution of the arrested person, or even of some other person altogether. This decision really provides that documents, even though illegally seized, may be put in evidence against an accused person.[13] But it may amount to a dangerous accretion of power in the hands of the police, even though it was made clear in the case itself that the accused would still have a right of civil action against the police for trespass etc in respect of any documents searched or taken away which proved to be of no use for a prosecution. This decision was to some extent superseded by the provisions in the subsequent Incitement to Disaffection Act 1934 and the Public Order Act 1936 which specify types of case in which it shall be lawful for the police to make searches without warrant. It should be remembered that many of the cases on this subject, and on that of police powers in respect of unlawful assemblies etc, considered below, took place in the economically and politically troubled times of the 1930s, when considerable difficulty was experienced in controlling the public meetings and activities of Communists and Fascists. Extensive powers were sometimes sorely needed. Concerning a more general run of criminal activity it is of note that the Theft Act 1968, s 25(3) provides that a person who is authorised to search premises for stolen goods may seize any goods he believes to be stolen, and that such seizure is legal whether or not the goods turn out in the end to have been stolen.

But *Kuruma v R* in 1955[14] makes it clear that the statutes leave untouched the basic common law provisions concerning

---

12   [1934] 2 KB 164, 103 LJKB 223.

13   An earlier case was *Jones v Owen* (1870) 34 JP 759. Later cases are *King v R* [1969] 1 AC 304, [1968] 2 All ER 610; *Ghani v Jones* [1970] 1 QB 693, [1969] 3 All ER 1700; and *R v Sang* [1980] AC 402, [1979] 2 All ER 1222. See also *R v Leatham* (1861) 8 Cox CC 498 at 503, where Crompton J said: 'It matters not how you get it; if you steal it even, it would be admissible in evidence'.

14   [1955] AC 197, [1955] 1 All ER 236.

admissibility of illegally obtained evidence. In that case a Kenyan had been found guilty, under Emergency Regulations in force at the time, of unlawfully possessing ammunition, and had been sentenced to death. Although he had been lawfully arrested under the Regulations, the policemen who arrested him had no power to search him, since they were below the rank of officer (assistant inspector) that had such a power to search without warrant in Kenya. Yet the policemen who arrested him did search him at the time of his arrest and they found two cartridges on him which were used as vital evidence at his trial. On appeal to the Privy Council, it was held that the use of such evidence was lawful, and of course any question of a right of civil action for any part of the search which proved useless for the purposes of a prosecution would have been small comfort to Kuruma. The Board, however, did direct that the sentence should not be carried out until the Secretary of State had had an opportunity of considering the case. A decision which possibly goes even further is *Chic Fashions. (West Wales) Ltd v Jones*[15] in which the Court of Appeal held that a constable who enters premises by virtue of a search warrant for stolen goods may seize not only the goods covered by the warrant, but also any other goods which he believes on reasonable grounds to have been stolen and to be material evidence on a charge of stealing or receiving against the person in possession of them or anyone associated with him. It was further held that subsequent events cannot affect the lawfulness of the original act, so that the fact that the goods were not stolen, and not used as evidence on the prosecution of any criminal charge, did not render the Chief Constable liable in damages for trespass. Clearly a balance should be struck between protection of the individual from excessive police powers and the desirablity of the police being able to use relevant evidence for a prosecution, however it is obtained. To take an extreme example, if a policeman chases a man he sees committing a theft, and in catching him happens to put his hand in the man's pocket, and then withdraws his hand which is (unlawfully) grasping a piece of paper, and this paper turns out upon inspection to be a written confession to a murder which the criminal had been carrying round with him for his own private

---

15 [1968] 2 QB 299 [1968] 1 All ER 229; see also *Malone v Metropolitan Police Comr* [1980] QB 49, [1979] 1 All ER 256.

delectation, it would be ridiculous to say that the policeman's only duty as far as the paper was concerned would be to return it and forget he had ever seen it. But on the other hand the police should not be encouraged to go to all sorts of unlawful lengths on the off-chance that some relevant evidence might turn up.

A further possibility of invasion of private premises by the police without warrant is instanced by the case of the *Thomas v Sawkins*,[16] which provides a limitation at common law upon the general right to hold a public meeting on private property. There it was held that the police may enter private premises without a warrant if they have reasonable grounds to believe that, if they are not present, seditious speeches will be made or breaches of the peace will take place. It appears, therefore, that a general licence to the public to enter private premises may be revoked as concerns anyone except a policeman, who may in his discretion override such a revocation. Such a police power is, however, limited, for it has also been held[17] that a power of entry without warrant does not exist where the commission or future commission of merely a summary offence has been suspected.

The cases considered above in this section are all cases at common law, but certain statutory powers of entry and search have also been conferred upon civil servants, public corporation officers, inspectors of gas and electricity meters, health visitors etc. The Criminal Law Act 1967, s 2(6), also permits a constable, for the purpose of arresting a person for an arrestable offence, to enter and search any place where that person is or where he has reasonable cause to suspect that person to be.

POSTAL INTERCEPTION AND TELEPHONE TAPPING

The interception of letters and particularly of telephone conversations has quite often been used as an aid to the maintenance of law and order. There have often been fears that the use of such a weapon could amount to a dangerous incursion upon normal civil liberties. But a Committee of Privy Councillors reported in 1957 that the opening of mail and tapping of telephones in certain circumstances for the defence of

---

16 [1935] 2 KB 249, 104 LJKB 572.
17 *Davis v Lisle* [1936] 2 KB 434, [1936] 2 All ER 213.

the realm was within the royal prerogative, as afforced by early statutory powers. The practice is under the control of the Home Secretary and requires his warrant. The Committee recommended that telephone messages should only be intercepted to detect serious crime or to safeguard the security of the state. In 1981 Lord Diplock, who had been asked by the Home Secretary to monitor the interception procedures, reported that they had been consistently used only within the limits suggested in 1957, and he recommended that no change in procedures or safeguards was required.

EMERGENCY POWERS AND MARTIAL LAW

Statutory emergency powers provide a further great infringement of personal and property freedoms. There is no need to consider them in detail here, for each such power is conferred for a particular purpose at a particular time, especially in war-time. The powers are thus of many different kinds and depend entirely upon the need which Parliament and the government feel has asserted itself at the time. They supplement, and in many ways supplant, such prerogative powers as exist to restrict individual liberty in times of stress.[18]

Martial law means the suspension of ordinary law, and the substitution therefor of discretionary government by the executive, exercised by the military. It is thought to be among the royal prerogatives to be able to proclaim martial law, though only in times of war. Such a power has not been exercised in England since the time of Charles I, and it is arguable that the prerogative has been superseded by parliamentary supremacy. Certainly it is most unlikely that the Crown should attempt to declare martial law, as Emergency Powers Acts are probably more efficacious. The Crown has, however, sometimes set up military tribunals under its prerogative power when a state of war existed, as for instance in Ireland in the early 1920s.[19] It is also conceivable that the parliamentary procedure might become impossible to work in the event of, say, a nuclear attack upon London without warning, but it might be more realistic to consider such a situation not as one where the prerogative power

---

18   See Chapter 3, above; eg *Case of the King's Prerogative in Saltpetre* (1607) 12 Co Rep 12.
19   See eg *Re Clifford & O'Sullivan* [1921] 2 AC 570.

came into its own, but as one where whoever was left alive would take upon himself the task of trying to restore some order out of the wreckage.

REMEDIES FOR WRONGFUL DEPRIVATION OF LIBERTY OR PROPERTY

Where there has been wrongful invasion of a person's liberty or property he may have any of the following remedies:

1 a civil action for damages, such as for assault, false imprisonment, malicious prosecution, trespass to the person, land or goods etc;
2 a similar action for recovery of property;
3 a criminal prosecution for assault, battery or theft etc;
4 a writ of habeas corpus to obtain his release from custody;
5 perhaps a prerogative order to quash a proceeding wrongly taken against him;
6 an appeal to a higher court, if the encroachment upon his liberty or property has been by court process; or occasionally
7 the right to take out a summons before a magistrate to recover costs of defending irregular and unjustifiable proceedings.

Of these remedies, the prerogative orders will be discussed in Chapter 11, and only habeas corpus requires any further explanation here.

HABEAS CORPUS

The prerogative writ of habeas corpus ad subjiciendum has for many centuries been one of the most important safeguards of individual liberty, and is still regarded as the ultimate weapon of defence for the oppressed.[20] The exact machinery and effect of the writ has been reformed by statute from time to time in order to ensure its full efficiency, the most notable of such statutes being the Habeas Corpus Acts of 1679 and 1816. An applicant for the writ must allege that he or the complainant is being unlawfully detained, whether it be for a criminal or civil offence,

---

20   It may perhaps be noted here that the right to habeas corpus has been suspended in Northern Ireland, where the executive has had certain powers of discretionary imprisonment, since 1939.

or for no offence at all (as, for example, where it is alleged that A is being prevented from leaving his own house by B). Frequently the application is made through an interested friend or relative of the imprisoned person. Probably the use of the telephone also plays some part today. A prima facie case must be made out before the writ will issue, but if a superior court or judge grants the issue of the writ the effect is to cause the alleged captor to 'bring the body' of the prisoner before the judge, who will then decide on the merits of the case whether there is any legal ground for continuing to detain him. If no such legal ground is found to exist the applicant is set free by the court. Until 1960, for example, it was not uncommon for persons detained in mental institutions to apply for the writ, and such applications were not infrequently successful because magistrates had exceeded their powers.[1]

If an application for the writ has been turned down, no second application will be entertained by any court in any circumstances on the same grounds unless fresh evidence is adduced. This rule was introduced by the Administration of Justice Act 1960 to resolve certain doubts which had persisted up to that time. In the same Act the opportunity was taken to widen the rules concerning appeals, which had previously only been possible in civil cases. Athough no appeal is permitted from the order of a single judge granting an application for habeas corpus in a criminal case, appeals *are* now permitted from any decisions of the Divisional Court, whether to grant or to disallow applications for the writ, and they lie, as in other criminal cases, direct to the House of Lords. But such appeals are not hampered by the necessity for the Divisional Court to certify that a case involves a point of law of general public importance which applies in other criminal appeals,[2] and so it is probably easier to appeal in a habeas corpus case than in any other criminal case. It is also provided that, although a single judge may grant an application for the writ, only the Divisional Court may refuse it,

---

1 Under the provisions of the Mental Health Act 1959 these powers of magistrates have now in effect been surrendered to the medical profession. Two doctors, one of whom must have special psychiatric qualifications, are empowered to order a patient's compulsory detention in hospital for a period of either 28 days or up to a year in the first instance. The patient has a right of appeal from such an order to a Mental Health Review Tribunal.

2 See Chapter 4, above.

so that any single judge to whom an application has been made, and who is disposed to disallow it, must refer the application to the full Divisional Court.

B. *Incursions upon freedom of assembly and association*

Although the practice of meeting or demonstrating peacefully in public is common and not in itself unlawful, there are a number of criminal offences which reduce the general freedom of assembly and association. The offences to be considered in this section are as follows:

(1) CONSPIRACY

A combination or agreement of two or more persons to do an unlawful act, or to do a lawful act by unlawful means, is an indictable offence at common law. Thus any assembly or association which amounts to a conspiracy will be criminal. Such assemblies must, however, be distinguished from the activities of Trades Unions, which are legal associations with the principal object of collective bargaining about wages and conditions of work.[3]

(2) AFFRAY

Where two or more persons engage in a fight, whether in a public place or on private premises, and thereby put other non-participants in fear, they are guilty of the common law offence of affray.

(3) UNLAWFUL ASSEMBLY

Where three or more persons either assemble to commit, or when assembled do commit, a breach of the peace, or assemble with intent to commit a crime by open force, or assemble for any common purpose, lawful or unlawful, in a manner which gives firm and courageous persons in the neighbourhood reasonable cause to believe that a breach of the peace will occur they are

---

3   Trade Union Act 1871; Trade Union and Labour Relations Act 1974.

guilty of a common law offence.[4] The distinction between this crime and that of conspiracy, apart from the requirement of at least three persons to form an unlawful assembly, is primarily that conspirators need not have caused any alarm to other people.

(4) ROUT

A common law rout is committed where persons unlawfully assembled are actually moving forward to the execution of their purpose.

(5) RIOT

A common law riot is committed where three or more persons, having a common purpose of a private nature, embark upon the execution of that purpose, with the intention of helping one another, by force if necessary, against anyone who may oppose them, and display such force or violence as to alarm at least one person of reasonable firmness and courage. Thus a riot may amount to the execution of the purpose of an already unlawful assembly.

(6) MISCELLANEOUS STATUTORY OFFENCES

It may be noted that the above crimes are usually committed in public places, and on this score they may be compared with police powers in respect of private premises, such as are exemplified in *Elias v Pasmore*[5] or *Thomas v Sawkins*,[6] discussed above. Various Acts of Parliament establish other offences, such

---

4 See eg the judgments in *Humphries v Connor* (1864) 17 ICLR1; *O'Kelly v Harvey* (1883) 14 LR Ir 105; *Wise v Dunning* [1902] 1 KB 167; 71 LJKB 165; cf *Beatty v Gillbanks* (1882) 9 QBD 308, where it was held not to be an unlawful assembly when the Salvation Army insisted on holding its normal peaceful procession in Wester-super-Mare, even though they had been ordered by the magistrates and the police not to do so because it was likely that it would be broken up by a rival 'Skeleton Army'. It may be noted that the crime of obstruction of the police, discussed below, was not thought at the time to cover the circumstances of a case where an assembly which the police wished to disperse may not in itself be unlawful: see T. C. Daintith 'Disobeying a Policeman—A Fresh Look at *Duncan v Jones*' [1966] PL 248; also W. Birtles 'The Common Law Power of the Police to Control Public Meetings' (1973) 36 MLR 587.

5 [1934] 2 KB 164, 103 LJKB 223.

6 [1935] 2 KB 249, 104 LJKB 572.

as unlawful drilling, seditious meetings, tumultuous petitioning, carrying an offensive weapon at a public meeting or in a procession, and wearing in any public place or at any public meeting a uniform signifying association with any political organisation or with the promotion of any political object. Only two such offences need be mentioned specially here, namely the offence laid down by section 5 of the Public Order Act 1936, and strengthened by the Race Relations Act 1976, s 70, and consisting of offensive conduct conducive to breaches of the peace, and incitement to racial hatred; and that of obstruction or assault of the police, now governed by the Police Act 1964, s 51.

Any person in a public place or at a public meeting who uses threatening, abusive or insulting words, or indulges in suchlike behaviour, or distributes or displays any writing, sign or visible representation of like effect, with intent to provoke a breach of the peace, or whereby a breach of the peace is likely to be occasioned, is guilty of an offence under section 5 of the Act of 1936. This section has been used by the police to prosecute those who publicly preach social hatred,[7] and the Public Order Act 1963 greatly increases the penalties which may be exacted by the courts. Provisions designed further to eliminate other aspects of racial discrimination are to be found in the Race Relations Act 1976, replacing earlier Acts of 1965 and 1968. Any person who wilfully obstructs a police officer in the course of his duty may be arrested without warrant. It is clear that this is a case where a policeman who has a suspicion that an unlawful assembly might take place can avoid having to wait and see, and can simply order the persons concerned to disperse. Any disobedience would then amount to obstruction.[8] But a decision in 1966 emphasises that obstruction of a police officer is not unlawful unless it is also wilful.[9] The appellant had been seen by a police officer acting suspiciously late at night in a district where a number of breaking offences had been committed on the same night. On being questioned, he refused to give his full name and address, to say where he was going or where he had come from, or to accompany the officer to a police box in order that his identity might be established. The Divisional Court held that he

---

7   See eg *Jordan v Burgoyne* [1963] 2 QB 745, [1963] 2 All ER 225.
8   As happened in *Duncan v Jones* [1936] 1 KB 218, 105 LJKB 71.
9   *Rice v Connolly* [1966] 2 QB 414, [1966] 2 All ER 649.

was entitled to refuse to do all these things until he had been arrested, that 'wilful' imported something done without lawful excuse, and that no obstruction without lawful excuse had been established in this case. Accordingly they quashed his conviction. Again it has been held that obstruction of a police officer is not in itself unlawful, giving rise to the right of the officer to effect an arrest without a warrant, unless the officer is actually acting in the execution of his duty.[10] And an assault upon a police officer in the execution of his duty is only committed, within the terms of the Police Act 1964, s 51, if the officer actually *was* executing his duty. Thus there is a good defence to such a charge if physical resistance is put up against police officers who are attempting to detain and search a person unlawfully.[11]

Once more the powers of the police are prominent as being the agency whereby the legal limitations are enforced. It will be noticed that, as before, much is left to the discretion of the individual police officer, and it may be argued that such exercise of discretion could be subjective. Police officers might be able to order law-abiding people to move away from a department store or a busy street for no apparent reason. Police are also much concerned with preventing and remedying traffic obstruction, and in enforcing local by-laws,[12] in both of which occupations they are empowered to exercise a wide discretion. Again, an officer might arrest without a warrant because he believed the individual arrested had committed an offence or was about to do so, or he might enter private property where he believed a breach of the peace was likely to take place, whereas no other reasonable policeman would have drawn the same conclusion, and it might be argued that such an arrest or entry would nevertheless be lawful. This solution would be undesirable, and although the point has not been decided directly it is probably correct to consider that belief in the commission or likely commission of an offence must be reasonable in the objective sense. Thus the policeman must behave as a 'reasonable policeman',[13] If this principle is accepted there is little danger

---

10   *Wershof v Metropolitan Police Comr.* [1978] 3 All ER 540.
11   *R v Waterfield* [1964] 1 QB 164, [1963] 3 All ER 659.
12   These are explained in Chapters 10 and 12, below.
13   Lord Hewart CJ, in *Thomas v Sawkins* [1935] 2 KB 249 at 254, [1935] All ER Rep 655 at 657, above, said: 'I think that there is quite sufficient ground for the

that the extensive police powers in this field of the law will ever be seriously abused.

C. *Offences against the state*

Any commission of a criminal offence amounts to an abuse of the limits of personal freedom permitted by the law, as also, in a different way, does the commission of any tort. It is not intended in this section to consider all criminal offences, but only those crimes against the state which are of such fundamental importance as to occupy a place in our constitutional law. Only three groups of these offences, treason, sedition, and offences against the Official Secrets Acts, need be discussed specially.

(1) TREASON

The most important statute concerning treason is the Statute of Treasons 1351, which is generally regarded as having been declaratory of the common law at the time, and which is still in force, although amended and added to in comparatively minor ways by subsequent Acts, primarily by statutes passed in 1702, 1707, 1795 and 1817. Under the Statute of Treasons the following types of conduct amount to the offence:

a Compassing the death of the King, the Queen or their eldest son and heir. An overt act is, however, necessary to prove the commission of this offence.
b Violating the King's consort, or eldest unmarried daughter, or his eldest son's wife.
c Levying war against the King in his realm.
d Adhering to the King's enemies in the realm, giving them aid

---

proposition that it is part of the preventive power and, therefore, part of the preventive duty, of the police, in cases where there are such reasonable grounds of apprehension as the justices have found here, to enter and remain on private premises . . .' See also *Piddington v Bates* [1960] 3 All ER 660, [1961] 1 WLR 162 (an appeal to the Divisional Court from conviction for obstruction of police officers in execution of their duty); and *Broome v DPP* [1974] AC 587, [1974] 1 All ER 314 (a trade union picket who had blocked the path of a lorry about to enter a 'blacked' building site, having failed to dissuade its driver from proceeding, and who also disobeyed a police order to move, was found guilty of obstructing the highway).

and comfort in the realm or outside. It has been held that the offence is committed whether the adherence is within or without the realm.[14]

e Slaying the Chancellor, Treasurer or the King's Justices, while in the discharge of their offices.

Two further types of treason added by later statutes are:

f Attempting to hinder the succession to the throne of any person entitled to succeed under the Act of Settlement 1701.

g Maintaining in writing the invalidity of the line of succession established by the Act of Settlement.

Treason is punishable by death,[15] and any prosecution for treason must be initiated within three years of the commission of the offence.

(2) SEDITION

A seditious intention is an intention to bring into hatred or contempt, or to excite disaffection against, the monarch in person, or the government and Constitution of the United Kingdom as established by law, or either House of Parliament or the administration of justice, or to excite subjects of the Crown to attempt, otherwise than by lawful means, the alteration of any matter in Church or state by law established, or to raise discontent or disaffection among subjects of the Crown, or to promote feelings of ill-will and hostility between different classes of such subjects. So runs the description given of it by Cave J in 1886.[16] Prosecutions for sedition are now rare, and are not normally instituted unless incitement to violence has taken place, but the term 'sedition' may cover any of three common law offences:

a Publication of a seditious libel, that is, publication in a permanent form of matter of a seditious nature.

---

14 *R v Lynch* [1903] 1 KB 444, 72 LJKB 167, where a British subject became a naturalised subject of the Boer Republic during the Boer War, and fought against the British. See also *R v Casement* [1917] 1 KB 98, 86 LJKB 467, where another British subject, during the 1914–1918 War, incited British prisoners of war in Germany to join the enemy forces and take part in an expedition against the British in Ireland; and *Joyce v DPP* [1946] AC 347, [1946] 1 All ER 186, discussed below.

15 This is now the only criminal offence in the United Kingdom for which the capital penalty remains.

16 *R v Burns* (1886) 16 Cox CC 355.

b Uttering of seditious words.

c Conspiring to do an act in furtherance of a seditious intention.

(3) OFFENCES AGAINST THE OFFICIAL SECRETS ACTS

Because the treasons listed as (c) and (d) above can only really be committed in war-time (the definition of an 'enemy' being a citizen of a country with which the United Kingdom is at war), it has been found necessary to legislate with respect to offences of spying and sabotage[17] in peace-time. The Official Secrets Act 1911 and 1920 make it an offence, inter alia,

a to approach, inspect or enter any prohibited place, ie an army or air force establishment, naval ship, arsenal etc,

b to make sketches or plans which might be useful to an enemy,

c carelessly to part with such documents, or to retain them longer than permitted,

d to communicate documents or information to any person which might be useful to an enemy,

e to obstruct any of Her Majesty's forces in the vicinity of any prohibited place, or

f to wear an unauthorised uniform, to make a false declaration or to forge a passport or permit in order in gain admission to a prohibited place.

The width of these provisions has often been criticised, and in 1972 a Departmental Committee headed by Lord Franks recommended some modification of the law intended to ensure that prosecutions should be confined to cases where the alleged acts of the accused concern matters of real importance. But no legislation to give effect to this recommendation has yet been introduced.

(4) MISCELLANEOUS OFFENCES

A number of other offences against the state should be borne in mind as of constitutional importance, but no attempt will be made here to explain or discuss them. The majority of them are statutory offences, and the list includes misprision of treason

---

17 The use of prosecutions under the Official Secrets Acts in order to deal with acts of sabotage as well as spying was made clear by the House of Lords in *Chandler v DPP* [1964] AC 763, [1962] 3 All ER 142.

(concealment of the offence of treason), attempts to alarm or injure the monarch, incitement to mutiny or disaffection, trading with the enemy, and offences against the Foreign Enlistment Act 1870.

ALLEGIANCE

In the case of treason and many of its kindred offences it is necessary before any prosecution can succeed that it should be proved that the accused owes allegiance to the Crown. The categories of persons who owe such allegiance are:

a British citizens,
b British dependent territories citizens, British overseas citizens and aliens resident in the United Kingdom, and
c British dependent territories citizens, British overseas citizens and aliens not resident in the United Kingdom, but who have previously been so resident, and have left either their families or their effects in the United Kingdom.

A short explanation of these three groups of persons is necessary.

(a) British Citizens. Until 1983 the attributes of British nationality were governed by many statutes, the most important of which was the British Nationality Act 1948. But a wholesale reform was effected by the British Nationality Act 1981, which came into force in 1983, and which fundamentally altered the basis upon which British citizenship is acquired. This ended some seven centuries of legal tradition under which birth in the kingdom gave an automatic right to citizenship, and replaced it with rules based much more on the continental system of citizenship by descent. Full British citizenship is thus now restricted to those with close personal connections with the United Kingdom, the Channel Islands and the Isle of Man. A child born in the United Kingdom will be a British citizen if the father or mother is a British citizen or is settled in the kingdom in the sense of being entitled to stay indefinitely. In addition there are detailed provisions concerning the acquisition of citizenship by descent, if a child is born abroad, by registration and by naturalisation. British citizens have full rights of entry into the United Kingdom and residence there.

The 1981 Act creates two other categories of citizen: (i) British dependent territories citizens, who are those living in the remaining British colonies, and who thereby have the right to enter and live in their own territories, but not in the United Kingdom; and (ii) British overseas citizens, who are those who were British subjects and citizens of the United Kingdom and colonies under the 1948 Act, but who have not become British citizens or British dependent territories citizens under the 1981 Act. British overseas citizenship carries no special rights.

Other Commonwealth countries have their own citizenship rules. Commonwealth countries for this purpose are the independent members of the Commonwealth discussed in Chapter 13 below, together with certain other countries which may not yet be fully independent, though independent in many respects, and which have been granted by the United Kingdom the privilege of possessing their own citizenship. It may be that a prime significance of this innovation in constitutional law is that, as far as the laws of the United Kingdom are concerned, only British citizens are now capable of committing treason by an act outside the United Kingdom and colonies, though there is as yet no case authority for this assertion. It is submitted that it is more accurate today to consider that for the purpose of the law of treason only British citizens owe permanent allegiance to the Crown, although in the more general law of the Commonwealth as a whole, discussed in Chapter 13, many other Commonwealth citizens owe allegiance to the Crown.

(b) and (c) British dependent territories citizens, British overseas citizens and aliens who owe temporary allegiance.   In view of what has just been said, citizens of other Commonwealth countries may be regarded as coming into the same category as British dependent territories citizens, British overseas citizens and aliens for the purposes of allegiance to the criminal laws of the United Kingdom, though not for all other purposes. The citizens of the Republic of Ireland, which is not a country within the Commonwealth at all, possess certain privileges under the terms of the Ireland Act 1949, and they are not for other purposes regarded as aliens, but again they come into the same category as aliens as far as the law of treason is concerned. Bearing this in mind, no explanation of the description 'aliens resident in the United Kingdom' is required here. But non-resident aliens under group (c) above need some attention. The authority for the existence of the group is a resolution of the English judges in

1707[18] to the effect that any alien who had once resided in Great Britain,[19] and who had then departed from the country, but leaving his family or estate behind him, could still be dealt with as a traitor if he should transgress the law of treason—provided he returned or was brought back within the jurisdiction of the courts, for the trial of an absent man for treason would be abortive. The meaning of this resolution seems plain, but it has probably been rather broadened in scope as a result of the case of *Joyce v Director of Public Prosecutions* in 1946.[20] In that case William Joyce, nicknamed 'Lord Haw-Haw' in the United Kingdom, was tried and convicted for treason on the ground that he had broadcast for and adhered to the German cause, while living in Germany during the Second World War. The commission of the treasonable act was beyond doubt, but the accused was in fact a citizen of the United States of America. Nevertheless the jurisdiction of the English courts was held to be valid because he had obtained a British passport by false representations, and had renewed it shortly before the outbreak of war. Yet he had left no family or belongings of any kind in this country, and the passport was not even found in his possession. The House of Lords came to its decision by a majority, Lords Simonds, Macmillan and Wright concurring with the speech of Lord Jowitt LC, while only Lord Porter dissented on the ground that the question whether Joyce was making use of his passport at the time of his broadcasts had not been drawn to the attention of the jury. Thus the principle in the judges' resolution of 1707 would seem to have been extended, and the decision is of the binding authority of the House of Lords, even though it has not infrequently been criticised. It is perhaps possible to suggest one reason for the decision which was not considered significant by the courts, namely that England was the locus of the crime, for although the treasonable acts were committed in Germany they would have had little point unless they were actually heard by listeners to the wireless broadcasts in England.

Apart from the law of treason and of certain other offences against the state, an alien in the United Kingdom enjoys full

---

18 Foster *Crown Law* p 183.
19 It will be recalled that the United Kingdom (then of Great Britain and Ireland) did not come into being until 1800: see Chapter 7, above.
20 [1946] AC 347, [1946] 1 All ER 186.

civic rights, provided his own country is at peace with the United Kingdom, although he may not own or have a share in a British ship or aircraft, nor may he vote or stand as a candidate in Parliamentary or local elections. The Crown may probably exclude aliens from the country whenever it wishes, under its Prerogative right, but in fact this is usually done, where necessary, by statutory provisions. Powers of internment and deportation are usually provided for by Act of Parliament. Enemy aliens can be arrested and imprisoned at common law, and they have no right to apply for a writ of habeas corpus against the Crown, or to bring civil actions, although they are permitted to defend civil actions or criminal prosecutions against them, and to appeal against adverse decisions of trial courts. There is legislation to control immigration to the United Kingdom from other parts of the Commonwealth, and to provide for deportation in certain cases. These provisions were considerably strengthened by the Immigration Act 1971, but the law is in fact similar to that enforced by many Commonwealth countries.

Powers of extradition are provided for by reciprocal treaties with various countries, whereby the United Kingdom government generally agrees (the exact agreement depends on the terms of each treaty) to hand over to such states any persons, whether British or not, either accused of or found guilty of committing any offences covered by the Extradition Acts 1870–1935. These Acts cover most criminal offences, except those which are of a political nature. Thus no extradition will be allowed where the case is really one of an individual claiming political asylum.[1] But the Suppression of Terrorism Act 1978 restricts the possibility of terrorists evading extradition by pleading that their crimes are political offences. Again, no extradition will be allowed where the accused has already been tried in the United Kingdom for the offence. The Fugitive Offenders Act 1967 similarly provides for the arrest and surrender of persons who are accused of having committed crimes in other Commonwealth countries, and who have fled to the United Kingdom.

---

1   As in *R v Governor of Brixton Prison, ex p Kolczynski* [1955] 1 QB 540, [1955] 1 All ER 31.

II. Duties of the Citizen in the United Kingdom

In the main body of this chapter the limitations upon the fundamental freedoms of the individual have been sketched. It is unnecessary to consider in any detail the constitutional duties of such individuals, because it can be appreciated that wherever the law has provided for a restriction upon full liberty it is the duty of all persons to obey that law. Similarly in respect of such freedom as remains after the restrictions upon it have been conceded, it is the duty of all persons to respect the individual liberties of others. Thus, to sum up, the laws of the United Kingdom provide for negative restrictions upon the safeguards for the constitutional rights of the individual. Such residuary rights must be respected by all persons, and can normally only be altered by Act of Parliament.[2] There is at once a privilege to enjoy these rights, and a complementary duty to respect them and to obey the law.

FURTHER READING

Clive Parry *Nationality and Citizenship Laws of the Commonwealth and of the Republic of Ireland* (2 Vols, 1957 and 1960)
Lord Denning *Freedom under the Law* (1949) Ch 2
K. C. Wheare *Modern Constitutions* (2nd edn, 1966)
Roscoe Pound *The Development of Constitutional Guarantees of Liberty* (1957)
I. Brownlie *The Law Relating to Public Order and National Security* (2nd edn, 1981)
H. Street *Freedom, the Individual and the Law* (5th edn, 1982)
D. Williams *Not in the Public Interest* (1965)
D. Williams *Keeping the Peace* (1967)
L. H. Leigh *Police Powers in England and Wales* (1975)
I. N. Stevens and D. C. M. Yardley *The Protection of Liberty* (1982)

---

2   Two other possible, though rarer, methods are delegated legislation (see Chapter 10, below) and judicial decisions. As regards the latter method it is arguable that courts only develop, rather than change, the law. This is perhaps a question of interpretation: see above, *Elias v Pasmore* [1934] 2 KB 164, 103 LJKB 223; and *Thomas v Sawkins* [1935] 2 KB 249, 104 LJKB 572.

Chapter 9

The Church

Complete religious toleration is practised throughout the United Kingdom and the British Isles, and citizens are free to join or support any religious sect they wish. The sole limitation upon the scope given to all religious bodies is that provided by the criminal law of the land. For example, although members of certain Eastern religions are permitted by their faith to practise polygamy, the contraction of a polygamous marriage in the British Isles amounts to the crime of bigamy; and it is no defence to such a charge that any second ceremony of marriage was performed according to bona fide religious beliefs.

Of the many churches which maintain a following in the British Isles, however, two occupy a certain more privileged position than others, namely the Church of England (Episcopalian) and the Church of Scotland (Presbyterian). These two churches are said to be 'established' churches, although this is not really a technical term and it does not imply that any other religious bodies, whether Christian or not, are in any way discouraged. In particular the Roman Catholic Church has many adherents, whilst several non-conformist churches, notably the Methodist, Baptist and English United Reformed Churches, have widespread national organisations, as has also the Episcopalian or Anglican Church in Scotland. Again, there are many adherents to the Jewish faith in the United Kingdom. The Church of Ireland (Anglican) was 'disestablished' in 1869 by the Irish Church Act, as was also the Church of England in Wales by the Welsh Church Act 1914, and thus they occupy a similar position in the eyes of the law to all other non-privileged religious bodies in the British Isles. It will be recalled from Chapter 2, however, that priests of the Roman Catholic Church and clergy of the Church of Ireland are barred from membership of the House of Commons, as are also clergy of the Church of England and ministers of the Church of Scotland.

The effect of 'establishment' differs slightly in each of the cases of the two churches concerned, and it is perhaps best to examine them separately.

I. The Church of England

The modern position of the protestant Church of England dates from the reign of Queen Elizabeth I, and in particular from the Act of Supremacy 1558 and the Act of Uniformity 1558, and its status was ratified in the Act of Union 1706. In a sense the Church was recognised by the state as being that which in its opinion truly taught the christian faith. As has been mentioned in Chapter 3, the monarch must be in communion with the Church of England,[1] and the monarch's accession declaration and coronation oath, and the whole form of the coronation ceremony, and of certain other ceremonial occasions, is according to the beliefs of the Church of England. Archbishops and Bishops of the Church sit in the House of Lords,[2] whereas no other church is officially so represented, although any priest or minister of the Church of England or of any other church who is also a peer may of course sit in the Lords. But perhaps the greatest effect of establishment has been that the decrees of the Church are of legal authority throughout England. Its legislative body is now the General Synod, instituted by the Synodical Government Measure 1969, and consisting of Bishops, clergy and laity. Any enactment which the Synod has decided to sponsor is formulated as a 'Measure', which is then submitted to Parliament for approval, such approval, if obtained, being given by simple affirmative resolution of each House of Parliament. Once a Measure has passed Parliament it takes effect as if it were an Act of Parliament, but it applies directly only to the Church of England, and will affect other persons or bodies only negatively or indirectly. The work of the General Synod is assisted by 43 diocesan synods.

The executive organisation of the Church is according to a hierarchy, with Archbishops and Bishops as the superior authorities, priests and deacons as the lower orders, and with the

---

1 Bill of Rights 1689, Coronation Oath Act 1688, and Act of Settlement 1701.
2 See Chapter 2, above.

monarch as 'Supreme Governor', though with no spiritual jurisdiction.[3] Many priests and deacons will, however, occupy posts of special ecclesiastical significance within a Bishop's diocese or within a local parish. Ecclesiastical courts or the Church of England are no longer of such general legal importance as they used to be before the middle of the nineteenth century, when they had competence in such matters as testamentary succession and matrimonial causes. Nowadays they have jurisdiction over internal ecclesiastical law only, usually concerning the interpretation of doctrine on the particular clerical behaviour of a clergyman. The hierarchy, composition and procedure of these courts was modernised by the Ecclesiastical Jurisdiction Measure 1963 (1963 No 1), but a final appeal in all matters still lies to the Judicial Committee of the Privy Council.

II. The Church of Scotland

The Church of Scotland is a protestant church, but with a non-episcopalian form of government. It received recognition in Scotland by a series of Acts of the Scottish Parliament before the union with England, and in the Treaty of Union 1706, and the ratifying statutes of the two Parliaments, the establishment of both the Church of England and the Church of Scotland was guaranteed permanently for the future, although, as we have pointed out in Chapter 2, Parliament cannot bind itself absolutely for the future as far as statutes affecting England are concerned: as we have seen, the position may be different in Scotland. The special constitutional position of the Church of Scotland does not conflict with the status of the Church of England, for the latter is established within England only. Whereas the Church of England has as its 'Supreme Governor' the monarch, who is also temporal head of the state, the Church of Scotland claims to exercise unfettered spritual sovereignty, and thus to possess a jurisdiction jure divino coordinate with that of the state. The legislative Acts of its General Assembly are regarded as statutes of the realm, needing neither parliamentary approval nor the royal assent.

---

3 Act of Supremacy 1558.

The organisation of the clergy of the Church of Scotland is not founded upon an hierarchical system, and thus there are no Bishops or other superior clergymen of the Church. The Church is governed by a hierarchy of courts, Kirk Session, Presbytery, Synod and General Assembly, in all of which ordained clergymen, called ministers, and lay elders have equal place. Each is presided over by a clerical Moderator, and the Moderator of the General Assembly ranks as the leader of the Church during his year of office. Although the monarch is not the 'Supreme Governor' of the Church, he or his Commissioner has the right to attend sessions of the General Assembly of the Church,[4] and it is conventional for him to attend services of the Church of Scotland when in Scotland. The Church courts enforce church discipline etc in much the same way as in the Church of England. The Church is entitled to legislate for itself, and does so normally through resolutions of its General Assembly[5] which, as has been pointed out above, do not require the approval of Parliament. It is perhaps for this reason that there is no direct representation of the Church in the House of Lords, as there is in the case of the Church of England.

It may therefore be seen that both the Church of England and the Church of Scotland maintain privileged positions in the constitutional system of the United Kingdom, but in effect their authority as established churches is restricted to England and Scotland respectively, and all churches are really of equal status in Wales and Northern Ireland.

FURTHER READING

Sir Thomas Taylor 'Church and State in Scotland' [1957] Juridical Review 121
R. King Murray 'The Constitutional Position of the Church of Scotland' [1958] PL 155
Sir H. W. Cripps *A Practical Treatise on the Law Relating to the Church and Clergy* (8th edn, by K. M. Macmorran, 1937)
E. Garth Moore *An Introduction to English Canon Law* (1967)

4　Act 1592, cap 8, of the Scottish Parliament (often referred to as 'the Charter of the Church'), which is still in force.
5　Church of Scotland Act 1921.

Part II

Principles of English
Administrative Law

Introduction

In the second part of this book we are only concerned with English law, rather than the general law of the United Kingdom. This is because, unlike other parts of constitutional law, administrative law has been built up in each of the component countries of the union as a separate and individual entity. No direct and apposite comparison can be made between the administrative laws of England and Scotland or Northern Ireland although it is true to say once more that the law of Northern Ireland is not greatly dissimilar from that of England.

The term 'administrative law' is difficult to define, for the scope of its subject has become very wide in recent years, and there is every indication that it will become even wider in the future. It may, however, be stated generally that it amounts to the law concerning the administration. This might have been a simple concept if it were not that the powers and sphere of influence of the administration in the United Kingdom today have spread so greatly to embrace almost every aspect of everyday life in the modern state.[1] Perhaps it is best to describe administrative law as that law which is concerned with any aspects of the administration of the country, and in particular the law governing the relationship between the state and the individual. In this latter respect it is inextricably bound up with the general law concerning civil actions, and it is for this reason above all that the administrative laws of the countries of the United Kingdom differ, for their general municipal laws have grown up separately.[2] It is submitted that English administrative law is of more widespread importance than the administrative laws of Scotland or Northern Ireland, for the

1 See Chapter 3, above.
2 See Chapter 1, above.

administrative laws throughout the Commonwealth are based upon it far more than upon the administrative laws of other countries in the union, and in any case the law of Northern Ireland in many ways reflects it. Scots administrative law is really the 'odd man out', and, as in numerous respects it defies comparison with the principles of the English law, particularly for example on the subject of remedies of the individual against the administration, which are quite distinct and cover different circumstances in Scotland from those in England, it is not intended here to indulge in any comparison of the two systems. This part of the book will be confined to English administrative law.

Chapter 10

Subordinate Legislation

It has been seen in Chapter 2 that in the United Kingdom the power to legislate is vested in Parliament at Westminster. This power is supplemented by the adjudicatory function of the law courts, which apply and interpret Acts of Parliament as may be necessary, but which also follow the rules established by the method of case precedent wherever no statute law is relevant.[1] But there is still another method of law-making, known as delegated or subordinate legislation, which stems from the position of Parliament as sovereign body, even though it is not a manifestation of the direct functioning of Parliament. Wherever an Act of Parliament provides that any government department, local authority, the Crown, or any individual or body shall have the power to make regulations or orders that shall have the force of law, that statute is regarded as laying down a method of creating delegated legislation, and any regulations or orders made under such powers take effect as if part of the 'parent' Act,[2] provided that they conform to the limitations expressed in that parent Act.[3] The power to legislate in this way may, however, be conferred only by an Act of Parliament, or, more rarely, by the royal prerogative. The term 'subordinate legislation' really includes law-making under the power of the royal prerogative, discussed above in Chapter 3, as where the Crown legislates by Proclamation or Order in Council for newly conquered or ceded colonies. But *delegated* legislation, properly so called, may only be created under statutory powers, and it is this subject which it is our main purpose to consider in the present chapter. Nevertheless, whether the authority for subordinate legislation be, in any particular instance, a statute or the royal prerogative, the person

1 See Chapter 4, above.
2 *Institute of Patent Agents v Lockwood* [1894] AC 347.
3 *Minister of Health v R, ex p Yaffe* [1931] AC 494, 100 LJKB 306

or body empowered to create the subordinate legislation is usually a part of the Crown, as we shall see presently, and thus the law concerning the effect and control of this legislation is administrative law. It may also be noted in passing that, in the case of delegated legislation, the parent Act may provide for sub-delegation of powers conferred, but that sub-delegation is only lawful if authorised expressly or by necessary implication by the enabling Act.

The necessity for the existence of subordinate legislation is primarily dictated by the exigencies of modern life in a democratic community. An enormous amount of regulation is required to ensure orderly and just provision for the needs of all citizens. There is far too much for Parliament alone to deal with in detail, and in any case some regulations have to be brought into force at very short notice in view of sudden changes of, for example, economic conditions. Parliament would be unlikely to be able to pass a Bill to meet such conditions sufficiently quickly, as its immediate programme of business may already be full. Again, the need for certain new regulations is often appreciated by government departments, which have special means of knowing the conditions prevailing in the country or the world in its own field of interest, but may not be apparent to MPs who are not members of the government or of that department, and who may belong to an Opposition party which would feel bound to oppose the measure for political reasons, as in the case of a Bill before the House. It has therefore become increasingly recognised by responsible persons during the past half-century that discretionary powers must be vested by Parliament in specific persons or bodies, though in most cases with careful safeguards to prevent abuse of such power. Although Lord Hewart severely criticised the growth of delegated legislation in his book *The New Despotism*, published in 1929 while the author was still in office as Lord Chief Justice of England, the fears that had prompted the publication were soothed by the later *Report of the Committee on Ministers' Powers* in 1932.[4] The result of this Report was that consistent opposition to the existence of the powers became less frequent, and the energies of those who had previously felt their danger were directed into reinforcing the safeguards surrounding the exercise of such powers.

4 Cmd 4060.

TYPES OF DELEGATED LEGISLATION

In effect it is open to Parliament to create any delegated legislative power it wishes, in whatever form and vested in whatever person or body it cares, for this is a power implicit in the sovereignty of Parliament. For example, it has sometimes conferred a power to impose taxation, or even to modify or adapt the parent Act or other Acts of Parliament, though Parliament will not normally do this without good reason. The most usual types of delegated legislation which have been provided for by statute in the past can be tabulated without great difficulty, and there is no reason to believe that Parliament will wish in the future to depart from its established practice. The main varieties are:

1 Local authority by-laws. Thus in statutes creating local authorities or in any way altering the powers of such authorities that already exist it is common to include a section or sections empowering the authorities to make local by-laws or regulations which shall have effect as binding law upon the persons in the district. An account of the system of local government will be seen in Chapter 12 below.

2 Public corporation by-laws. The nature of public corporations has already been described in Chapter 3, and the power of these corporations to make by-laws for the regulation of their business, employees etc is similarly frequently included in statutes creating them or altering their powers.

3 Rules of the Supreme Court and of the County Court etc. Rules committees are sometimes set up by statute specifically empowered to make rules concerning the practice and procedure of the courts already described in Chapter 4.

4 Regulations made by the European Commission or the Council of Ministers.

5 Ministerial or departmental regulations. These, together with the delegated legislation in category (6) below, are the most common and widely used of delegated legislative powers, and they are called statutory instruments. This is why delegated legislation falls under the heading of administrative law, even though in theory such a power to create legislation may be conferred by Parliament upon anyone, and not just upon the administration.

6 Orders made by the Monarch in Council. These are often similar in nature to ministerial or departmental regulations, but they are generally of wider national importance, and the authority for their creation may stem from the royal prerogative as well as from Parliament. Instead of being formulated entirely by the minister or government department primarily concerned, without any outside help or advice being necessary, they may originate as the embodiment of government policy, but must receive the assent of the monarch in the Privy Council before they may come into effect. In practice the distinction between Orders in Council and ministerial or departmental regulations is perhaps not vital, because a normal meeting of the Privy Council will consist of the monarch, three or four ministers who are Privy Councillors, including the Lord President of the Council, and the Clerk to the Privy Council, but the procedure does at least ensure slightly more publicity and the possibility of second thoughts on the part of the government.

It will be realised that in the case of the last two types of delegated legislation any powers which are conferred by statute will enable the government of the day to enforce its policy decisions as being law, which could result in a grave abuse of the trust imposed in the executive. But the responsibility of ministers to Parliament is an important check on any such tendency, even though it would probably be possible for the government to force any Bill embodying its desires through Parliament by means of its party majority if it really wished. The executive control of, or at least predominance of power in, Parliament would lead to the same policy becoming law, but the advantages of delegated legislation from the point of view of the government are those of speed, especially in emergencies or in war-time, the ability to deal with a technical subject-matter without having to explain the whole issue painstakingly to Parliament, and flexibility, in that regulations may be made, altered or rescinded as and when it is thought appropriate and without unnecessary delay. To set against these advantages it may be urged that the lack of general publicity consequent upon dealing with such matters in the ordinary legislative form in Parliament may be harmful and unfair, but certain safeguards have been brought into being to counteract any such undesirable trends.

A. *Parliamentary safeguards*

(1) LAYING BEFORE PARLIAMENT

In order to provide that Parliament shall at least have cognisance of such delegated legislation as is of national importance, namely Orders in Council and ministerial and departmental regulations, the enabling Act very often now provides that any regulations made under the terms of the Act, or any draft Orders in Council which are proposed, shall be laid before Parliament or before one or other of the Houses of Parliament.[5] In many cases there is no express power vested in the House or Houses by the enabling Act to vote on the matter, and thus the 'laying before' is purely for the information of members; and in some cases indeed the delegated legislation may already have come into force. Members may, however, ask parliamentary questions concerning the instrument, even though it is not possible for the House to vote on the matter directly. On the other hand it is sometimes provided that the regulation shall not come into force or continue in force unless an affirmative resolution of one or both of the Houses shall have been passed, or else that the regulation or order shall become or remain law unless one or other House annuls it by a negative vote within a specific time. It must be emphasised that the specific kinds of 'laying before' under the principle discussed here may theoretically be limitless in number, because in each case the nature of the control depends upon the terms of the parent Act. But the Report of the Select Committee on Delegated Legislation in 1953 declares that there are only three types of 'laying before' in practice, namely those already mentioned:

a the laying of an instrument before either or both of the Houses for information, Parliament having no power under the terms of the parent Act to vote on the instrument;

b the laying of an instrument before either or both of the Houses, with the requirement of an affirmative resolution to bring it into force or to continue it in force; and

c the laying of an instrument before either or both of the

---

5 To the author's knowledge there has never yet been a statutory provision that an instrument should be laid before the House of Lords only, but in principle there is no reason why such a provision should not be enacted.

Houses, with the possibility (but no requirement) of a negative vote which would annul it or prevent it coming into force.

(2) THE SCRUTINY COMMITTEES

A Special Orders Committee was set up in the House of Lords in 1925, charged with the duty to scrutinise and report upon instruments requiring an affirmative resolution of the House before coming into effect or continuing in force, ie instruments laid before the House which fall under heading (b) above, but not those falling under (a) or (c). A Select Committee on Statutory Instruments was also set up in the Commons in 1944 as a delayed implementation of one of the recommendations of the Committee on Ministers' Powers.[6] 'Statutory instruments' is a collective term which covers all Orders in Council made under statutory powers (as opposed to those made under the prerogative power), together with such ministerial or departmental regulations as may be designated statutory instruments by their enabling Acts, but not other varieties of delegated legislation. The Committee was empowered to scrutinise a wider range of instruments, and to report upon many matters of form, though not of policy. It is perhaps a tribute to departmental integrity and conscientiousness that the Committee only found it necesary to draw the attention of the House to a few out of the total number of instruments referred to it, but it was also wasteful of time for the two Houses to maintain separate scrutiny committees.

In 1973 these two committees were in effect merged to form a new Joint Committee on Statutory Instruments which is charged with the duty to consider all instruments or draft instruments laid before both Houses of Parliament. It must report to both Houses, and draw their attention to any such secondary legislation which (i) imposes a tax on the public, (ii) is made in pursuance of an enactment containing specific provisions excluding it from challenge in the courts, (iii) purports to have retrospective effect where there is no express authority in the

---

6 Cmd 4060 (1932), pp 67–69.

enabling statute, (iv) has been unduly delayed in publication or laying before Parliament, (v) has come into operation before being laid before Parliament and there has been unjustifiable delay in informing the Speaker of the delay, (vi) is of doubtful *vires* or makes some unusual or unexpected use of the powers conferred by the enabling statute, (vii) calls for any special reason of form or purport for elucidation, or (viii) is defective in its drafting. The older Select Committee on Statutory Instruments still remains to scrutinise those few instruments which, under the terms of the enabling Acts, are to be laid only before the Commons. But otherwise the Joint Committee has superseded the older bodies. Further, the Commons at the same time set up a Standing Committee of the House to consider statutory instruments and draft instruments referred to it on the question of merits.

In 1974 the Commons also set up the Select Committee on European Secondary Legislation, and the Lords set up the Select Committee on the European Communities. These Committees are charged with the task of singling out and bringing to the attention of Parliament the more important Community proposals. The Commons Committee in any case makes a general report to the House on Community business every six months. Provided these Committees make their views clear in sufficient time, a debate on a matter of urgency or importance can take place in Parliament before the Council of Ministers makes a final decision.

(3) OTHER PARLIAMENTARY SAFEGUARDS

Additional parliamentary safeguards are inherent in the power of members of either House to ask questions concerning, inter alia, delegated legislation, to call for a debate (probably through the Leader of the Opposition), and even in extreme cases to move the censure of the government. Such procedures may be particularly useful in respect of delegated legislation in the form of statutory instruments which only have to be laid before Parliament, or one of the Houses of Parliament, for information, and where consequently there is no possibility of a direct affirmative or negative resolution, ie instruments falling under heading (a) above.

B. Judicial Safeguards

If any delegated legislation, of whatever kind, is formulated contrary to the terms of its enabling Act, or in excess of the powers conferred, then it may be challenged in the courts as being ultra vires the enabling Act. The actual methods whereby such challenge may be pursued will be considered in the next chapter, but for the present it is sufficient to say that although delegated legislation takes effect as if it is part of its parent Act,[7] and is thus of statutory force, yet this result does not come about unless the delegated legislation is intra vires, that is, properly formulated according to the terms of the Act.[8] Although Acts of Parliament are immune from judicial challenge, delegated legislation can be challenged in the courts on the ground that it is ultra vires, and this may include the power of the courts to hold delegated legislation bad as being unreasonable.[9]

C. Political Safeguards

It may sometimes be provided in the parent Act that the minister concerned should consult interested bodies or an Advisory Committee before issuing regulations. Again, the Statutory Instruments Act 1946 provides that all statutory instruments shall be published by the Stationery Office after they have been made. Where any statutory instrument is required to be laid before Parliament after being made, the published copies must contain the date on which it came or will come into operation. Such provisions are useful in ensuring a reasonable amount of consultation before committing a policy to become law, and in making provision for any interested party to be able to read the terms of the instrument concerned, but they are perhaps not strictly methods of control. But any person charged with an offence under a statutory instrument has a good defence if he can prove that the instrument had not at the time of

---

7 *Institute of Patent Agents v Lockwood* [1984] AC 347.
8 *Minister of Health v R, ex p Yaffe* [1931] AC 494, 100 LJKB 306; *R v Halliday, ex p Zadig* [1917] AC 260. See also *Allingham v Minister of Agriculture* [1948] 1 All ER 780, where an invalid sub-delegation of power had been made.
9 See eg, *Kruse v Johnson* [1898] 2 QB 91.

the offence been published by the Stationery Office, unless reasonable steps had been taken to bring the instrument to the notice of the public, the person charged or persons likely to be affected by it.[10]

It is possible that some additional method ought to be devised to bring instruments to the notice of the general public more readily than by publications of the Stationery Office, although it may be unrealistic to imagine that an apathetic populace would avail itself of such wider publicity. The present provision for publication of statutory instruments does at least provide for *some* publicity of the measures concerned, and thus it may facilitate one final safeguard against unwarranted acts of the executive, namely that of public opinion. Great unpopularity may make it politically expedient for the government to change its policy and to rescind any regulations already made.[11] This is essentially a topic outside the scope of a lawyer, but it is possible that such a political safeguard is a real supplement to the existing legal safeguards, and that it ensures that the legitimate purposes of delegated legislation are not misused to any serious extent.

FURTHER READING

H. W. R. Wade *Administrative Law* (5th edn, 1982)
J. F. Garner *Administrative Law* (5th edn, 1979)
D. C. M. Yardley *Principles of Administrative Law* (1981)
S. Bailey, C. Cross and J. F. Garner *Cases and Materials on Administrative Law* (1977)
Sir Carleton K. Allen *Law and Orders* (3rd edn, 1965)
D. Foulkes *Administrative Law* (5th edn, 1982)

---

10 Statutory Instruments Act 1946, s 3(2).
11 An instance of the effect of public opinion (although not a case of delegated legislation) was the agitation leading to the setting up of a Public Inquiry into the Crichel Down affair in 1954; see *Public Inquiry ordered by the Minister of Agriculture into the disposal of land at Crichel Down*, Cmd 9176 (1954).

Chapter 11

Tribunals, Inquiries and the Control of Power

Administrative law, as has been said at the beginning of Part II of this book, is a special sub-division of constitutional law, and there has been an increasing tendency in this century for it to be made to cover a number of topics and problems which fall outside the ordinary scope of the common law courts. It is for this reason that many so-called administrative tribunals have been set up to deal with such subjects. Departmental inquiries may also take place before an administrative decision is made. In the previous chapter we have seen how the administration frequently has subordinate legislative powers conferred upon it. But administrative law is also concerned with executive and judicial powers of the administration. We have already described in Chapter 3 how the Crown exercises its executive functions directly, and it is now our task to consider the tribunals and authorities which have been set up for the purpose of dealing with various aspects of administrative law, and which have either executive or judicial functions, and sometimes a mixture of the two. The Crown is the embodiment of the administration as a whole, but its function is not ended there: it is a subordinate legislature, acting under powers conferred by Act of Parliament or by the royal prerogative, and it also exercises judicial powers, as conferred upon it from time to time by Parliament. Yet there is a clear division between the position of administrative authorities, other than the Crown direct, acting in executive or judicial capacities and other authorities acting as subordinate legislatures, for executive and judicial powers are often conferred upon tribunals separate from the Crown, even if appointed by the Crown, whereas only the Crown itself or some part of it has ever had the power to exercise all three functions conferred upon it by Parliament. It is for this reason that subordinate legislation has been considered separately in the last chapter, while the powers of tribunals, other than the Crown, are considered here.

We shall examine first administrative tribunals, then inquiries, and finally the methods of control by the ordinary courts of law both of tribunals and of the Crown and other administrative authorities.

I. Administrative Tribunals

Most administrative tribunals are set up by Act of Parliament or under powers conferred by statute, and their composition depends upon the statutory terms governing them. It would probably be more accurate to designate them as 'statutory tribunals', since their powers are mainly judicial rather than administrative, but the traditional term is now so well established that the use of any different description would only serve to confuse. It may be asked why there is any need for such tribunals, since pure administration can normally be carried out by the Crown or its servants, and judicial decisions can be obtained through the ordinary courts of law. The answer to this question is that there are nowadays too many problems of law and administration for the courts to cope with effectively, and the pure administrative functions of these tribunals are really subsidiary to their judicial functions. The number of cases involving these problems is enormous, and the requirements in dealing with such problems are mainly speed, cheapness, a special aptitude for the particular type of problems concerned (a quality provided for by the composition of each tribunal), lack of formality and forms, and in most cases the provision of rough and ready justice. Tribunals of various kinds are far more readily adapted to these needs than are the ordinary courts, and thus for the most part are able to perform their tasks to the greatest advantage of the various parties concerned. Many of the existing tribunals have in the past been severely criticised, largely, it is submitted, because of the previously widespread practice of not publishing their decisions or giving reasons for their decisions, and also partly in ignorance of the valuable work which is done by tribunals with little or no fuss or publicity. It is, however, true to say that certain tribunals have on occasions committed serious errors either of law or judgement, and these have received publicity. Criticism of administrative tribunals was among the reasons leading to the setting up of a Committee on

Administrative Tribunals and Enquiries, under the chairmanship of Sir Oliver Franks, which reported in July 1957.[1] The majority of the recommendations of this Committee were accepted by the major political parties, many were implemented by government departments as matters of policy, and a Tribunals and Inquiries Act 1958 was passed to provide for the enactment of such of the recommendations as required immediate statutory effect. This statute, together with certain amendments and additions, has now been re-enacted as the Tribunals and Inquiries Act 1971.

Detailed criticisms of administrative tribunals have in the main been three-fold:

a That they are totally unnecessary. This criticism has probably been finally answered by the findings of the Franks Committee that they are absolutely necessary, and even desirable, in modern conditions,[2] though some methods of control should be strengthened. The Committee also emphasised that the three great principles which should always be followed by such tribunals were those of openness, fairness and impartiality. On the whole these principles have usually been observed in the past, and it is clear that they are carefully followed today.

b That a system of entirely separate administrative courts should be set up, rather like the French system of courts concerned only with the *droit administratif*, or alternatively that there should be set up an Administrative Appeal Court or an Administrative Division of the High Court, to hear appeals direct in all cases from administrative tribunals. The Franks Committee decided against these suggestions, but it did, as we shall see presently, recommend an extension of the possibilities of direct appeal. Despite the Franks Committee there remained for 25 years a considerable body of opinion among English lawyers favouring at least the creation of an Administrative Division of the High Court.[3] It seems, however, that these views have now been substantially met by the setting up in 1982 of a special panel of judges of the

1   Cmnd 218.
2   Cmnd 218 (1957), paras 403, 406.
3   See eg *Administration under Law* (a Report by Justice, 1971).

Queen's Bench Division to sit in the Divisional Court when it is hearing any case involving administrative law.

c That all administrative procedure should be standardised, as in the United States of America, where there is a federal Administrative Procedure Act, passed in 1946. This Act has been only partly successful, because of the great diversity of work covered by administrative agencies, and the Franks Committee probably extracted the value from this criticism without adopting it in toto, by recommending the setting up of a Council on Tribunals to keep a watchful eye upon the procedure of the various tribunals, and to recommend changes where it thinks fit.

It is not usually necessary for a law student to have any detailed knowledge of the various types of tribunals, and fuller lists, including the detailed duties and powers of each tribunal, may be studied elsewhere,[4] In this book we are concerned only with principles, and it should be noted that tribunals may be of any kind at all. Whatever their composition or detailed powers they will be regarded as administrative tribunals provided that their functions in some way involve a consideration of the relationships of or disputes between the state and the individual.

Examples are the General Commissioners of Income Tax, the Lands Tribunal, Independent Schools Tribunals, Local Valuation Courts and Mental Health Review Tribunals. There are also some tribunals which are set up to deal with disputes which arise between individuals, and which are in fact of little or no interest to the state as such so far as their individual decisions are concerned. Examples would be Rent Tribunals and Rent Assessment Committees. In some foreign countries, such as France, it is very doubtful whether this latter group of tribunals would be considered as dealing with anything outside the realm of ordinary private law,[5] but they are still regarded as administrative tribunals in this country because they deal with subjects which are outside the scope of the common law courts, and which are an integral part of the broad social policy of the country. It is probably also correct to consider the Restrictive

---

4 Eg Sir Carleton K. Allen *Administrative Jurisdiction* (1956), reprinted from [1956] PL 13; and the Annual Reports of the Council on Tribunals.

5 See C. J. Hamson *Executive Discretion and Judicial Control: an Aspect of the Conseil d'Etat* (1954).

Practices Court, created by the Restrictive Trade Practices Act 1956, as an administrative tribunal, even though it contains judges of the High Court (in addition to other non-lawyer members) who are not sitting by virtue of their offices in the High Court, and who, when sitting, do not wear wigs or gowns. The Patents Appeal Tribunal has a somewhat similar composition, and, as its title shows, is actually designated a tribunal.

A number of matters concerning tribunals generally may be briefly noted:

1 Following the Franks Committee recommendation, a Council on Tribunals now advises the Lord Chancellor as regards England and Wales and the Lord Advocate as regards Scotland upon the general supervision and procedure of tribunals and inquiries, and makes reports to Parliament upon its work.

2 Chairmen, and in certain other cases the members, of tribunals are normally selected by the appropriate minister from a panel of persons appointed by the Lord Chancellor.

3 Chairmen of tribunals generally have legal training.

4 Legal representation is normally allowed, if required by any of the parties who appear before tribunals.

5 There is a full disclosure of all material facts to all parties before a tribunal hearing, and adequate notice of such a hearing is given.

6 Hearings are held in public, unless public security is involved or intimate personal or financial matters, or professional capacity or reputation, are concerned.

7 Reasons for decisions must be given, if requested.

8 The Franks Committee recommended that there should normally be an appellate tribunal to hear appeals on fact, law or the merits from any first instance tribunal, but that otherwise no special appeal tribunal or court should be set up. This particular recommendation has never yet been implemented. It is, however, submitted that it is hard to visualise any useful way in which appeals on *fact* can lie to an appellate tribunal without such an appeal developing into a simple rehearing of the issue which was heard below. If that were to happen the tribunal hearings would be robbed of their virtues of speed and cheapness. From such an appellate

tribunal, when constituted, the Committee recommended that there should be an appeal on law only to the Divisional Court (or the Court of Session in Scotland). Although the Tribunals and Inquiries Act did not institute appeals to an appellate tribunal, it did provide for appeals on law to lie from most tribunals to the Divisional Court (or Court of Session). The effect of the enactment, therefore, is to provide for appeals on law to the court in the case of most of the tribunals from which such appeals did not already lie.[6]

9 Appellate tribunals now usually publish selected decisions for the guidance of lower tribunals. It may be stated with some confidence that since the implementation of most of the Franks Committee's recommendations there is no longer any substantial reason for dissatisfaction with the powers and duties of tribunals.

II. Inquiries

Where Parliament has decided to entrust the power to make decisions concerning aspects of administrative law to some person or persons independent of the administration it will normally confer this power on a tribunal. But much decision-making affecting the administration is retained in the hands of ministers and their departments. It is, however, quite common for a statute to provide that a minister may only make a decision after first following a procedure intended to enable those who will be affected by his decision to make their views known; and this procedure is called an inquiry. The most usual inquiries are concerned with proposals which affect private property rights, and so inquiry procedures are used, for example, in connection with schemes to create new towns, appeals to the minister against refusal by a local planning authority of proposals to develop land, and proposals to acquire private land compulsorily for housing, or in order to build airports or new motor-

---

6 See *Rule of Law* (Conservative Political Centre, 1955) Appendix, in which are listed the most important tribunals from which appeals of various kinds, either to a court or to another tribunal or to the minister, already lay before the Act.

ways. The inquiry is conducted by an inspector, who must be careful to allow all objectors a fair chance to put their case, and the inspector then makes a report and recommendations to the minister.

The Franks Committee, which has already been referred to, was required to consider the system of both tribunals and inquiries, and a number of the reforms subsequently effected have concerned the latter. (It is curious that the Committee was asked to deal with 'Enquiries', whilst Parliament then legislated for 'Inquiries'!) The most far-reaching reform stems from the provision, now in the Tribunals and Inquiries Act 1971, that the Lord Chancellor may make rules regulating the procedure to be followed where any inquiries are held on behalf of a minister, and such rules have been made covering a number of the most common types of inquiry, particularly those held before a minister decides on the merits of appeals to him against local refusal of planning permission. These rules now specify the period of notice to be given before an inquiry is held, the procedure to be adopted at the inquiry, the form of the inspector's report to the minister, and the way in which the minister's eventual decision, together with reasons, must be notified to the parties concerned. In particular it is provided that where a minister differs from the inspector on a finding of fact, or takes into account any new issue of fact, and is in consequence disposed to disagree with any recommendation made by the inspector, he must give the parties who appeared at the inquiry an opportunity of making representations or of having the inquiry reopened before he makes any decision contrary to the inspector's recommendations. It will be readily seen, therefore, that the ministers are far less free than they were before the Franks Committee reported to make decisions in this field which pay scant regard to the weight of evidence at prior inquiries. Perhaps the trend of greater control over the powers of ministers is in this area taken to its fullest extent by the provisions, in the Town and Country Planning Act 1968, for the final determination by the inspector himself of a number of appeals against the refusal of planning permission. This effectively removes the decision-making power from the minister altogether, even though this provision was really made to relieve the department of a flood of minor appeals.

III. Judicial Control: Grounds

In the previous chapter it was stated that a consideration of the detailed procedure for judicial control of delegated legislation would be deferred until the present chapter. It is now our task to explain the procedures which are used not only for the judicial control of delegated legislation, but also for the control by the courts of administrative tribunals, inquiries and various powers exercised by the Crown, and sometimes also for more general purposes in purely private law, a problem which does not concern us here. It is proposed first to describe briefly the grounds upon which judicial control may be exercised, and then to list and describe the actual remedies which are used.

The grounds for judicial control are basically three in number:

1 That the jurisdiction of the tribunal or other administrative authority was defective. This is generally called the ultra vires doctrine, but there are many different ways in which it may be invoked. Thus an act may have been done by the wrong authority; or the authority may not have been properly appointed or constituted; or the authority may have exceeded its power; or some fact which is a condition precedent to the possession of power by an authority may have been absent; or power may have been exercised in bad faith, unreasonably, for an improper purpose, or after taking irrelevant considerations into account.

2 That the authority acted in breach of natural justice. There are two distinct rules of natural justice, namely:
   a that each interested party must have been heard, after being properly acquainted with any case that has been made against him; and
   b that an authority must act in the absence of any reasonable suspicion that it was biased, or had any substantial personal, pecuniary or proprietary interest in a dispute before it.

3 That the authority acted in error of law. Some errors of law committed by, say, a tribunal may well go to jurisdiction, but it is also possible to be in error of law while nevertheless acting properly within jurisdiction. As we shall see in the next section of this chapter, it is possible to sue the Crown directly in tort,

and in such cases also it would seem that the essential basis of the suit is that the Crown has acted in error of law.

In recent years the courts have made it clear that anything done ultra vires or in breach of natural justice is void, while an error of law within jurisdiction merely renders whatever has been done voidable, and thus needing to be quashed. It used to be thought that judicial control of administrative authorities was only possible where they were under a duty to act judicially, but the House of Lords decided in the important case of *Ridge v Baldwin* in 1963[7] that the courts were free to examine any act by such an inferior authority, and to set it aside if one of the grounds for judicial review was established. In any event it has long been accepted that delegated legislation may be set aside if it should prove to be ultra vires.

IV. Judicial Control: The Remedies

The actual remedies by which judicial control may be achieved may be divided into two main groups, those which are direct and those which are indirect.

A. Direct remedies

The direct remedies in this field are primarily either appeals (provided by the statutes governing the various tribunals and other authorities) or actions for damages. But it should also be noted that a defence to a prosecution for an offence under delegated legislation may well take the form of an assertion that the regulation concerned is ultra vires. This, if successful, would be a particularly direct form of remedy.

It is not necessary to explain the nature of an appeal, and the identity of the courts or bodies to hear appeals from tribunals will depend upon the terms of the various statutes. But from most tribunals for which no appellate structure already existed the Tribunals and Inquiries Act 1971, s 13 (re-enacting a provision in the earlier 1958 Act), provides that an appeal on law

---

7 [1964] AC 40, [1963] 2 All ER 66.

lies direct to the High Court. Nor is it intended here to explain the elements of an action for damages which will lie wherever a tort has been committed or there has been a breach of contract. It is most unlikely that such an action would be appropriate against a tribunal not directly connected with the Crown, which can rarely be a party to a contract or commit a tort. It may well be possible, however, that grounds for actions for damages may from time to time arise against ministers (sometimes deciding matters after inquiries) or other servants of the Crown. Until the passage of the Crown Proceedings Act 1947, actions in tort were not available against the Crown, and actions in contract could only be brought after a petition of right had been granted by the Crown itself, the petition having the effect of giving permission to the aggrieved person to bring his action. Some attention must therefore be accorded briefly to this statute and the resultant legal position.

THE CROWN PROCEEDINGS ACT 1947

Section 1 provides in effect that any person or body may bring an action in contract direct against a government department, except in three types of case. The exceptions are cases in which the Crown remains privileged from legal actions for damages, or for the recovery of a liquidated sum, or for injunction or specific performance, and cover contracts dependent upon a future grant of money from Parliament (for no litigant can be allowed to force Parliament to grant funds to enable the government to carry out its contractual obligations), contracts which fetter future executive action,[8] and contracts of service with members of the armed forces.[9] Thus, to take an example from the last exception, no soldier has the right to sue the Crown for wrongful dismissal, or

---

8 It is not really clear what this phrase means. There are very few direct cases upon the point: see J. D. B. Mitchell *The Contracts of Public Authorities* (1954); D. Foulkes *Administrative Law* (5th edn, 1982) pp 342–348; D. C. M. Yardley *Principles of Administrative Law* (1981) Ch 5.

9 The position is now rather different in the case of contracts of service with civil servants. The Industrial Relations Act 1971, ss 22 and 162, re-enacted by the Trade Union and Labour Relations Act 1974, s 1 (2) and Sch 1, para 33, provides for a procedure before an Industrial Tribunal in cases of alleged unfair dismissal of employees, including Crown servants. Under the Employment Protection Act 1975 provision is also now made for an order of reinstatement or re-engagement, and for an award of compensation. But there is still no provision for action to be taken by civil servants against the Crown in the courts by traditional legal process.

for reduction or arrears of pay. The reason for this is that the armed forces are still under the prerogative power of the Crown, as has been seen in Chapter 3, except in so far as funds for their upkeep etc must be provided annually by Parliament.

Section 2 provides that actions in tort may now be brought directly against government departments or against the Crown as a whole, although only in specific circumstances, namely:

1 in respect of torts committed by its servants or agents,
2 in respect of any breach of duties which a person owes to his servants or agents at common law by reason of being their employer,
3 in respect of any breach of the duties attaching at common law to the ownership, occupation, possession or control of property, or
4 in respect of a breach by the Crown of statutory duties, even though the common law presumption that the Crown is not bound by statute is still applicable unless excluded by the statutes concerned expressly or by necessary intendment.

On reflection it is a little difficult to understand quite what this section was intended to mean, as it is hard to imagine the Crown committing any tort, except through a servant or agent, particularly since section 40 of the Act preserves the immunity of the monarch personally from any liability in law. But, whether by design or not, it seems plain that the true meaning of the section as enacted is to provide a general right of action in tort against the Crown wherever the Crown has been responsible for the commission of any tort whatever, except in specified instances set out in later sections. But any further consideration of the section must be deferred until the reader has consulted more detailed works upon the subject.[10] The common law personal liability of Crown servants of course remains untouched in any way by the Act. Such servants are personally liable for any injuries they commit for which they are unable to produce legal authority.

The remaining sections of the Act provide for certain special matters either not covered by the two general sections or

---

10 See eg, G. L. Williams *Crown Proceedings* (1948); H. Street *Governmental Liability* (1953); G. H. Treitel 'Crown Proceedings: Recent Developments' [1957] PL 321; and the textbooks and sourcebooks on administrative law.

exceptional to them. There is no need to examine them fully here, but in particular it is enacted that the Crown is not liable for the death or personal injury of a member of the armed forces on duty caused by any other such member of the armed forces (section 10). As regards this latter situation, the Admiralty Board or a Secretary of State may, if satisfied of the facts, issue a certificate that the persons concerned were on duty as members of the armed forces, and this certificate is final and may not be questioned in any court of law. The Crown may now be ordered to produce documents relevant to any particular case (section 28), although the privilege to withhold such documents where a minister certifies that their production might be injurious to the public interest is still left to the executive. 'Crown privilege', as it has usually been called, used to be accepted by the courts virtually without restriction, but in 1968 the House of Lords held that courts have the power to disallow any such claims of privilege, and to order the production of the documents concerned.[11] A court should not order the production of Cabinet minutes, or of documents the disclosure of which would be contrary to national security. But, subject to such judicial self-discipline, a court will now make a more objective inquiry into whether the public interest against disclosure outweighs the other public interest that in the administration of justice the eventual decision should be based on all the relevant facts. 'Public interest privilege' has in effect replaced the older 'Crown privilege'.[12]

Thus, although there are still exceptions and reservations, the Crown is now far nearer the position of a private contractor, employer or occupier of premises as far as litigation is concerned than it was before 1947. To this extent English law has approached more nearly to the concept of the rule of law favoured by Dicey, and discussed above in Chapter 5.

---

11 *Conway v Rimmer* [1968] AC 910 [1968] 1 All ER 874. In *R v Lewes Justices, ex p Secretary of State for Home Department* [1973] AC 388 at 400, 406, 412, the House of Lords described the phrase Crown privilege as 'wrong', 'misleading', 'not accurate' and 'a misnomer', though in the event the claim to withhold from disclosure a confidential police report was allowed.

12 See eg *Burmah Oil Co Ltd v Bank of England* [1980] AC 1090, [1979] 3 All ER 700.

B. Indirect Remedies

(1) THE PREROGATIVE ORDERS

Since the middle ages the superior courts of law (now the High Court in England) have possessed three methods of controlling the exercise of jurisdiction in inferior courts or bodies, and tribunals and inquiries of all kinds now come into the latter category. These methods of control were known as the prerogative writs, and their nature is essentially the same today, although their procedure was simplified by the Administration of Justice (Miscellaneous Provisions) Act 1938, s 7, so that they have now become prerogative orders. Each will be explained very shortly.

(a) Certiorari.   Any party who believes himself aggrieved by the proceedings of an administrative authority may apply to the High Court for a certiorari.

If any one of the alleged grounds for judicial control is proved to the satisfaction of the High Court, the proceeding below is quashed. Error of law on the face of the record of the inferior authority is no longer such a common ground for certiorari in practice as it was before direct appeals from most tribunals to the High Court on points of law were established by the Tribunals and Inquiries Act 1958 (now 1971), but it remains important for the review of cases decided by tribunals, such as Mental Health Review Tribunals, from which no such appeal yet lies. But it should be noted that no alternative decision on the merits is made by the High Court in a certiorari case, thus distinguishing the effect of this remedy from that of appeal.

(b) Prohibition.   This order is similar in most respects to certiorari, except that its effect, if granted, is to prevent a case from being heard or continuing before, say, a tribunal, rather than to quash what has already taken place. Thus it is sought at an earlier stage in the proceedings before the tribunal, but the grounds for its issue are similar, even though it is rare, if possible at all, that an error of law can be alleged, because the record of the issue is not yet completed below.

(c) Mandamus.   Whereas the two previous orders are negative in effect, mandamus is positive, for if granted it has the effect of ordering the tribunal to do something. It may be sought, for

example, where a tribunal has refused to hold a proper hearing, or where a minister has failed to carry out a public duty or exercise a discretion entrusted to him.[13] But it will not lie against the Crown, or against any servant of the Crown to order him to perform any duty owed exclusively to the Crown.

All three of these remedies are regarded as 'last resort' remedies, for it is possible that a statute may have laid down a method of appeal from the particular tribunal concerned, in which case that course must be followed to the dissatisfaction of one of the parties before a prerogative order may be granted.

(2) OTHER INDIRECT REMEDIES

(a) Declaration. A simple declaration of the law upon a particular point may sometimes be an appropriate remedy against an administrative authority. No declaration may be sought, however, unless the point at issue is a real, and not theoretical, one; and a possible drawback to the remedy is that there is no method whereby it may be enforced, since the issue before the court is not strictly a 'live' dispute. All other judgments may always be enforced by attachment for contempt, but there is no direct method of coercing a party against whom a declaration has been obtained. It may be that disobedience would lead to a later direct action for damages or an injunction, in which the law would already have been decided, and only the facts would have to be proved. In any case it is possible to obtain a declaration in conjunction with some other positive remedy, such as an award of damages or an injunction, and there appears to be no record of a case in which a declaration has been disobeyed. But a court has refused a declaration where such a non-coercive remedy would be ineffective, as where the complaint was not that a tribunal had acted ultra vires, in which case its decision would be a nullity, but merely that it had made an error of law within the confines of its jurisdiction, which has been held to make the decision voidable.[14] It would not be possible for such a tribunal to reopen the matter unless its original decision had been *quashed.*

---

13 Eg in *Padfield v Minister of Agriculture, Fisheries and Food* [1964] AC 997, [1968] 1 All ER 694.
14 *Punton v Ministry of Pensions and National Insurance (No 2)* [1964] 1 All ER 448, [1964] 1 WLR 226.

(b) Injunction.   This remedy has the effect of forbidding the doing of something, as being illegal. Thus it in many ways substantially resembles prohibition, but it is not used so often against administrative tribunals. Its most common use in the field of administrative law is against so-called 'domestic tribunals', such as disciplinary committees (eg of the Jockey Club), which are set up for internal purposes within a profession or a club, rather than by statute, or against trade unions.[15]

(3) APPLICATION FOR JUDICIAL REVIEW

It can readily be seen that English administrative law has included a veritable patchwork of remedies, and in recent years it has been thought by most lawyers that the procedure for obtaining any one or more of these remedies should be reformed and simplified. A Report published in 1976 by the Law Commission, on Remedies in Administrative Law,[16] recommended a new procedure which was then substantially implemented by amendments to the Rules of the Supreme Court coming into effect in 1978. It is now provided that any person considered by the court to have sufficient standing in a matter may, as an alternative to applying for an individual remedy only, make what is termed 'an application for judicial review'. In his application he may ask for certiorari, prohibition, mandamus, declaration or an injunction, or any combination of them. The application must normally be made to the Divisional Court of the Queen's Bench Division, which in its discretion may make such order as it thinks fit as a result, and may also award damages where appropriate, though it may refuse to grant any application that is unduly delayed. The new rules eliminate several procedural defects surrounding the old remedies, and in particular provide that where the relief sought is certiorari the High Court may remit the matter to the court, tribunal or authority below with a direction to reconsider it, and to decide the matter in accordance with the findings of the High Court. It seems likely that these reforms will prove to be a significant improvement in administrative law, and that applications for

---

15   Eg as was attempted in *Gouriet v Union of Post Office Workers* [1978] AC 435, [1977] 3 All ER 70.
16   Cmnd 6407.

judicial review will virtually replace the older procedure of applying for individual indirect remedies. This is especially so because the Rules prescribe that in an administrative law case an application for one or more of the prerogative orders may now only be made by the new procedure; and the courts have in recent cases taken the view that applications for declarations and injunctions in administrative law cases should also be by the same route.

V. Extra-judicial Remedies

In the field of pure administration there has been a growing feeling that the citizen requires some further safeguard to his liberties and rights in addition to the traditional parliamentary question and the doctrine of ministerial responsibility to Parliament. The Parliamentary Commissioner Act 1967 was passed in response to this feeling, and it establishes for Great Britain a Parliamentary Commissioner for Administration, modelled on the Scandinavian office of Ombudsman.[17] The Commissioner is appointed by the Crown and holds office until he is 65, being otherwise removable only in consequence of an address from both Houses of Parliament, so that his tenure of office is protected in the same way as that of the superior judges. He may, on a complaint being referred to him in writing by an MP, investigate any action taken by or on behalf of a government department or certain other listed authorities, if there is no court or tribunal in which such action may reasonably be challenged. Cabinet papers are exempt from any investigation, but otherwise the Commissioner's powers to search and question are wide. He is empowered to investigate any complaint that injustice has been sustained in consequence of maladministration within the powers of the department or other authority. Maladministration usually takes the form of such things as bias, neglect, delay, incompetence, failure to explain adequately, inattention, perversity, turpitude or arbitrariness. The Commissioner has no power to enforce any

---

17 The first such office to be created in the Commonwealth was in New Zealand in 1962. A Parliamentary Commissioner was also established in Northern Ireland in 1969.

decision he may arrive at, but he must report his results to the MP and government department concerned, and may also report to Parliament. Furthermore his periodical reports are received by one of the Select Committees of the House of Commons, which will then pronounce its own opinion on the issues he reports upon.

Although the first two holders of this office interpreted their powers somewhat restrictively, the third Commissioner, Sir Idwal Pugh, who preferred to be described as the Parliamentary Ombudsman, in a number of ways broadened the scope of his work. This trend has been continued by the fourth Commissioner, Sir Cecil Clothier QC, who was appointed in 1979, and who became the first British Parliamentary Ombudsman to be a lawyer and not a former civil servant.

The Ombudsman is now a valuable aid towards keeping the proper balance of power between the citizen and the state. Three National Health Service Commissioners, one each for England, Wales and Scotland, started work in 1974, all three offices currently being held by Sir Cecil Clothier along with his main office as Parliamentary Commissioner.

Three Commissions for Local Administration, again one each for England, Wales and Scotland, were established by the Local Government Act 1974 and the Local Government (Scotland) Act 1975, to investigate complaints of maladministration by local authorities.[18] The overlap between some of the holders of these various offices may help to provide continuity and consistency in reports and decisions. The Police Complaints Board, established in 1976, which has already been mentioned in Chapter 3, bears a close relationship to the other avenues for extra-judicial remedy dealt with in the present chapter, though there is considerable pressure at the present time for the independent element in the investigation of complaints against the police to be strengthened. Professional bodies now also have independent officers who investigate and report upon complaints made about the profession or its members. An instance of such an officer is the Lay Observer, appointed under the Solicitors Act 1974, who may investigate

---

18   The appointment in 1982 of the present author as Chairman of the Commission for Local Administration in England in effect produced the second United Kingdom lawyer Ombudsman, though other Commissioners for Local Administration in England and Wales had been former local authority chief executives with legal training.

complaints about the Law Society's handling of complaints against solicitors.

FURTHER READING

H. W. R. Wade *Administrative Law* (5th edn, 1982)
J. F. Garner *Administrative Law* (5th edn, 1979)
D. Foulkes *Administrative Law* (5th edn, 1982)
D. C. M. Yardley *Principles of Administrative Law* (1981)
S. Bailey, C. Cross and J. F. Garner *Cases and Materials on Administrative Law* (1977)
S. A. de Smith *Judicial Review of Administrative Action* (4th edn, by J. M. Evans, 1980)
P. P. Craig *Administrative Law* (1983)
The Annual Reports of the Council on Tribunals
The Reports of the Parliamentary Commissioner for Administration
Law Commission Report on Remedies in Administrative Law, Cmnd 6407 (1976)

Chapter 12

Local Government

The machinery for the government of local areas throughout the United Kingdom is almost entirely separate from that of the central government, though always subject to the overriding powers of Parliament by statute or, where appropriate, of the central government. It is of course possible and proper for the government of the whole country to exercise such powers as it possesses by virtue of Acts of Parliament or the royal prerogative in such a way as to affect local areas of the Kingdom in various different ways. But, subject to such exercise of power, the different local authorities are independently empowered to carry out and enforce executive duties within their particular districts. They may also legislate upon certain matters within their jurisdiction, and all these powers are derived either from Acts of Parliament or from Royal Charters granted under the royal prerogative.[1] The exercise of the prerogative in this field is regulated by statute, and the powers of local authorities are mostly contained in the London Government Act 1963 and the Local Government Act 1972. It is our purpose in this chapter to outline the types of local authorities which exist at the present time, and their various powers. The authorities listed below are those which exist in England and Wales, all of which are under the general supervision of the Secretary of State for the Environment, although this does not mean that he necessarily wields great arbitrary powers over them. The local authorities in Northern Ireland are not dissimilar in the main, and elections for the recently reformed Northern Ireland district councils were first held in 1973. They are under the supervision of the Secretary of State for Northern Ireland. The new regional and district authorities in Scotland, and the all-purpose authorities of

1 And see Chapters 3 and 10, above.

148

Orkney, Shetland and the Western Isles, started work in 1975, and are supervised by the Secretary of State for Scotland. It may be noted that, in Northern Ireland, elections for the district councils and for the European Parliament (as a result of the European Assembly Elections Act 1978) are held by proportional representation, ie members of political parties are elected in similar proportion to that of the votes cast. Elsewhere in the United Kingdom all elections are conducted according to the principle that the winner is whichever candidate receives the most votes.

I. The Types of Local Authorities

The local authorities of England and Wales may be divided up as follows:

(1) THE LOCAL AUTHORITIES OF LONDON

The local government organisation in the London area was reorganised by the London Government Act 1963. Greater London consists of the City of London, the 32 London Boroughs, the Inner Temple and the Middle Temple. Greater London now includes areas which were previously parts of surrounding counties, but it is possible that the Act of 1963 does not go far enough, in that it fails to take account of large areas in surrounding counties where many working Londoners live. The authorities of Greater London are as follows:

(a) The Greater London Council. This consists of a chairman and councillors. Originally there were also aldermen, but, under the terms of the Local Government Act 1972 aldermen were abolished with effect from 1977. Councillors are elected every four years, and the chairman is elected annually by the council. The GLC is perhaps the most powerful of all the local authorities in the country, because of the vast population within London. It has extensive powers over metropolitan roads, planning, reserve housing, main sewerage, sewage disposal, fire protection, ambulances and civil defence. A committee of the GLC, known as the Inner London Education Authority, administers the education service within the area occupied by the 12 'Inner London Boroughs'.

(b) London Borough Councils   There is one council for each of the London Boroughs, and each consists of a mayor and councillors, aldermen having been abolished with effect from 1978. The mayor is elected annually by the council, and the councillors are elected in a similar way to those in the GLC. The powers of these councils cover such subjects as local health, sanitation, the provision of public baths and libraries, children, and the collection of rates, which are in effect local taxes. The 20 'Outer London Boroughs' are also education authorities.

(c) The City of London Corporation   This body corporate came into being as a result of prescription over a long period of history but its powers have been regulated from time to time by Royal Charters and by statutes. It may be regarded as roughly of parallel status to the London Borough Councils, and its functions are exactly the same. The government of the corporation is carried on through three 'Courts' or councils, the Court of Common Council, the Court of Common Hall and the Court of Aldermen. It is not necessary here to consider further their exact functions or composition, but the various representatives who sit in these Courts are the Lord Mayor of London, aldermen, common councilmen, the two Sheriffs and certain liverymen of the ancient City Companies of craftsmen and tradesmen.

(d) The Benchers of the Inner and Middle Temples   Certain minor local government functions are still exercised by the benchers of these two Inns of Court, and the London Government Acts 1939 and 1963 recognise that the Temples are within Greater London, but outside the City and the London Boroughs. This is a traditional status, for which there appears to be no real legal foundation, other than prescription or custom,[2] but it is of little importance in practice, as the inhabitants of the area are nearly all barristers in their chambers, very few of whom actually reside in the Temple.

In addition to the authorities so far listed, there are a number of separate authorities administering services which, outside London, are sometimes the concern of local authorities. These include the Metropolitan Water Board, the Thames Water

---

2   But see Williamson *The History of the Temple, London* for further information.

Authority, the Port of London Authority, and the London Transport Board.

(2) LOCAL AUTHORITIES OUTSIDE LONDON

Outside London the structure of local authorities is uniform and governed by the Local Government Act 1972. The present authorities were elected for the first time in 1973, and took over their full powers on 1 April 1974. In effect the country is for local government purposes covered by a three-tier system of authorities, governing respectively counties, districts and parishes. But six of the counties are designated as metropolitan counties, because they cover areas of the greatest concentration of population and industry, such as the West Midlands and Merseyside. In these counties there are metropolitan districts, the authorities for which have rather greater powers than those in non-metropolitan districts. The three types of authorities are as follows:

(a) County councils. Each council consists of a chairman and councillors, all of whom are elected for four years, and all of whom retire at the same time. The next election for these councils will be in May 1985. Each council has a number of powers exercised concurrently with district councils, such as the control of museums and art galleries, swimming baths, parks and open spaces, tree preservation, and many aspects of town development. But the county council has exclusive powers over such matters as structure plans for the county, highways, traffic, consumer protection and refuse disposal. County councils outside metropolitan areas also have exclusive powers over the very important matters of education, youth employment, personal social services and libraries.

(b) District councils. Each county is divided into a number of districts, each of which has its own council, consisting of a chairman and councillors. Each member is elected for four years, but normally one-third of the council will retire every year, except for a year in which a county council election is to be held. Any district council or London Borough Council may, however, opt for the whole council to be elected together every four years, and many districts, including all the London Boroughs, have so opted. As well as the powers exercised concurrently with county

councils, district councils have exclusive powers over such matters as housing, planning development control, building regulations, markets and fairs, local licensing, refuse collection, clean air and home safety. Metropolitan district councils also have exclusive powers over education, youth employment, personal social services and libraries.

(c) Parish councils and meetings.   All parishes in rural areas have parish meetings, which consist of a chairman and all the local government electors of the parish, and which must meet at least once a year. Such parishes with a population of 300 or more must also have a parish council (and parishes with a population of under 300 may elect to have a parish council), consisting of a chairman, elected annually, and councillors, elected for four years and retiring in rotation. A council has slightly greater powers than a meeting, but the powers of each cover such subjects as the maintenance and signposting of footpaths and bridleways, and parks and open spaces.

In all these authorities, except parish meetings, members are directly elected by the people, and the abolition of aldermen in the GLC and the London Boroughs completes this pattern for the whole country. But councils have the power to recognise service to local government by conferring the title of 'honorary alderman' upon suitable persons. Non-elected members may be co-opted to committees. Special provisions enable any district council for an area which was previously a borough by Royal Charter to retain its previous status, together with the title of mayor for its chairman. Similarly a petition may be submitted, and will be favourably considered, to enable any district to retain any special distinction or title, such as 'Royal Borough', 'City', 'Lord Mayor' or 'Sheriff'.

Of more fundamental importance, the Local Government Act 1972 extends the right of the public and press to attend council meetings and meetings of all committees of local authorities. Councillors now receive a taxable flat-rate attendance allowance when on council business. Local Government Boundary Commissions have also been set up on a permanent basis to review local government boundaries and electoral arrangements.

It will be seen from the above that the local administration of each part of England and Wales is accounted for by a greater and a lesser authority, neither of which is a national body. But the central government does have certain supervisory powers over these authorities, which are conferred by Act of Parliament. It is not necessary here to examine the supervisory powers closely, for they are of different kinds created under different statutes, but primarily this control exists because all local authorities receive financial grants from the Treasury to supplement rates levied and to pay for such local administration as cannot be afforded by the local funds. It is therefore easy to appreciate that the government will only initiate or support legislation in Parliament to provide for such financial grants when the local authorities affected have behaved in a proper manner in the immediate past, and seem likely to continue to do so. Sometimes the Secretary of State is empowered to make discretionary grants or to supervise the local authorities in certain ways according to his discretion, and then the exercise of such discretion will depend even more upon the 'good behaviour' of the authorities concerned. Further reform of the financing of local government is expected shortly, but in certain ways the 1972 Act has provided local authorities with greater financial freedom than hitherto. It can also be seen that, just as Parliament is able to control the functions and even the existence of local authorities by virtue of its legislative supremacy,[3] so it may also delegate powers of administration or legislation to the central government and to the local government authorities.[4] The powers of the latter are both administrative and legislative, with the restrictions discussed already in Chapter 10.

It is not proposed to discuss further in this chapter the powers of local authorities over the police, upon which the reader will find an account in Chapter 3 above. There is also no need to deal specifically with the powers to create committees or appoint officers (such as Chief Executive Officers), all of which depend on their governing legislation.

II. Who Elects Members of Local Authorities?

Since the Representation of the People Act 1949, now replaced by the Representation of the People Act 1983, the franchise for

---

3 See Chapter 2, above.
4 See Chapters 10 and 11, above.

local government elections has been practically equated to that existing for Parliamentary elections, even though it is not quite identical. The right to vote is possessed by all British citizens or citizens of the Republic of Ireland of full age who are (1) not subject to any legal incapacity,[5] and (2) either resident in the area on the qualifying date,[6] or, if not so resident, who occupy as owners or tenants any rateable land or premises in the area of the yearly value of not less than £10. Thus there is an alterntive occupation qualification for those who cannot satisfy the residence qualification. Peers also have the right to vote in local elections.

Since the local government reorganisation of the past few years, party politics have come to play almost as great a part in local government elections as they do in national elections, and most candidates for election now stand as party candidates. In many ways the growth of the party political element in local government is regrettable, since the problems for any administrative sub-division of the country are practical everyday ones rather than questions of national importance, and there are all too many examples of experienced and hard-working local councillors who lose their seats solely because of the temporary swing of the political pendulum against their own party. But on the other hand social policy is bound to play a certain part in the duties of such authorities, and there may be some advantages in groups of council members having a worked-out and agreed policy on such issues. It is of course to be hoped that the size of grants to local authorities from the Exchequer will not be influenced to any measurable extent by the political bias of the central government in relation to local authorities dominated by members of their own or an opposition party.

FURTHER READING

C. A. Cross *Principles of Local Government Law* (6th edn, 1981)
W. E. Hart and W. O. Hart *Introduction to the Law of Local Government*

---

5 See Chapter 2, above. The legal incapacities are the same as for national elections, save that peers may vote in local elections.

6 10 October in each year, the annual register of electors being published the following 15 February: Electoral Registers Act 1953.

and Administration (9th edn, by Sir W. O. Hart and J. F. Garner, 1973)

Davies *Local Government Law* (1983)

R. M. Jackson *The Machinery of Local Government* (2nd edn, 1965)

P. W. Jackson *Local Government* (3rd edn, 1976)

J. A. G. Griffith *Central Departments and Local Authorities* (1967)

R. J. Buxton *Local Government* (2nd edn, 1973)

Lord Redcliffe-Maud and B. Wood *English Local Government Reformed* (1974)

Part III

The Commonwealth

Chapter 13

The Commonwealth

I. The Concept of the Commonwealth

The Commonwealth of Nations, formerly known as the British Commonwealth or, at an even earlier period, the British Empire, is an unique institution in the world, binding together in a loose and flexible way a great number of countries of different kinds. Some of these countries are independent and sovereign states, while others are subordinate in some way to one or other of the independent countries, usually to the United Kingdom. The independent countries used to be known in British constitutional law as Dominions, but are now simply styled independent or full members of the Commonwealth, enjoying equal rights and privileges with the United Kingdom. Subordinate members of the Commonwealth are of various types which will be considered in the course of this present chapter.

II. The Independent Members of the Commonwealth

The independent members were all originally dependent upon the United Kingdom, or, later upon another independent country within the Commonwealth, but have attained their status at different times. Canada was the first to gain full responsible government, ie the power to legislate was vested, by Royal Instructions to the Governors of Upper and Lower Canada, in local institutions which were fully representative of the local inhabitants, and it became the Dominion of Canada by virtue of the British North America Act 1867 (though the term 'Dominion' did not at that time have the meaning later accorded to it by the Statute of Westminster 1931, which is discussed below). From the existence of this legislative power and the practice of ministerial responsibility to Parliament arose the institution of a responsible executive in the North American colonies themselves, rather than in Wesminster. By 1931 Canada had been joined by Australia, New Zealand, the Union of South Africa (now a republic outside the Commonwealth), the Irish Free State (now the Republic of Ireland, and also outside the Commonwealth) and Newfoundland (which is now the tenth Province of Canada). Up till that time they held the status in British constitutional law of internally self-governing colonies, and as such were independent for most practical purposes, but still subject to the control of the United Kingdom in a few respects. But by the Statute of Westminster 1931 the Dominions were granted full legislative independence, being responsible for all legislation affecting both their own internal and external affairs. Executive powers were still vested in the royal prerogative, regulated by convention, in all the Dominions, just as in the United Kingdom, but this prerogative power is exercised by the Crown as represented by the government of the country concerned, and not by the United Kingdom government. In any case the legislature of each Dominion, parallel with the United Kingdom Parliament as regards the government in the United Kingdom, as has been seen in Chapter 3, now had the power to override the royal prerogative by statute should it wish to do so. From 1931, therefore, the previous jurisdiction of the United Kingdom Parliament over the Dominions ceased, except for certain special purposes to be discussed shortly concerning Canada and Australia. The only legal links of a tangible kind which remained were the common allegiance to the British Crown, meaning in this context the monarch, and the continued jurisdiction of the Judicial Committee of the Privy Council as ultimate appellate tribunal from courts throughout the Commonwealth outside the United Kingdom.[1] The independent members have the power to break even these two remaining links, by reason of their complete legislative independence of the United Kingdom, while still electing to remain full members of the Commonwealth, though it should be remembered that, in view of the absolute equality of status now existing between the United Kingdom and the other full members, any such decision to revoke the common link of

---

1   The Judicial Committee of the Privy Council is discussed in Chapter 4, above.

allegiance to the Crown, but still to remain a member of the Commonwealth, must be accepted by all the other members. On the analogy of a club with no specific rule for the alteration of its present rules, any one member would probably be able to black-ball another member which desired to alter its status yet again, but still remain a member.

The term 'Dominion', which was used in the Statute of Westminster to denote the independent members of the Commonwealth, has now fallen out of use, because of the possible colonial ring in its sound. What would previously have been known as Dominions are now called full members or independent members of the Commonwealth.

It seems that the granting of independence by the United Kingdom to a country which previously possessed the status of, for example, a colony is a question for the United Kingdom government and Parliament alone.[2] But the approval of all the existing independent members must be obtained before the newly independent nation may take its place in the Commonwealth as an equal with the existing members.[3] The same principle will apply in the case of the granting of independence to any of their dependencies by other full members of the Commonwealth. Australia and New Zealand, for example, have a number of dependencies which may be affected in this way. The full members of the Commonwealth which have attained their status since 1931 (and in fact all of them since the Second World War), and which have joined the 'Club' of the United Kingdom, Canada, Australia and New Zealand, are India, Sri Lanka (formerly Ceylon), Ghana, Malaysia, Cyprus, Nigeria, Sierra Leone, Western Samoa, Jamaica, Trinidad and Tobago,

---

2 But see the section of this chapter dealing with associate states, below. Rhodesia made a unilateral declaration of independence in 1965, but this was not recognised by the United Kingdom or by other members of the Commonwealth. In 1970 Rhodesia also purported to become a republic. However the force of world opinion eventually led to a settlement agreed by all parties in 1979 under which the former colony became the independent republic of Zimbabwe.

3 See the statement of Mr (later Sir) Winston Churchill to the House of Commons on 16 June 1952, 502 HCDeb778; also S. A. de Smith 'The Independence of Ghana' (1957) 20 MLR 347 at 352–354. It may be noted that at the time of the passage of the Ghana Independence Act 1957 there was some apprehension that South Africa might oppose the new nation's full membership of the Commonwealth because of the colour question, but these fears proved groundless. Further difficulties over racial problems were averted for the time being by South Africa's withdrawal from the Commonwealth in 1961.

Uganda, Singapore, Kenya, Tanzania, Malawi, Malta, Zambia, the Gambia, Guyana, Botswana, Lesotho, Barbados, Mauritius, Swaziland, Tonga, Fiji, Bangladesh, the Bahamas, Grenada, Papua New Guinea, the Seychelles, the Solomon Islands, Tuvalu, Dominica, St Lucia, St Vincent, Zimbabwe, Kiribati, Vanuatu, Antigua, Belize, Nauru, the Maldives, Brunei, and St Christopher and Nevis.[4] It is possible that a few more dependencies will achieve this status before the list can be regarded as complete. The independent republic of Nauru was, in 1968, granted 'special membership' of the Commonwealth. This includes the same rights to participate in Commonwealth affairs as other independent members, but not the right to be represented at meetings of Commonwealth heads of government. Other Commonwealth countries which have taken advantage of this special membership are Tuvalu, St Vincent and the Maldives. It is unnecessary, for the purposes of an introductory book restricted to British constitutional law, to embark upon a discussion of the detailed constitutional organisation of any of these independent members of the Commonwealth, though it may be noted that, in distinction from the United Kingdom, the constitutions of these countries are, with the partial exception of New Zealand, to be found in specific constitutional documents. This is logical, for whereas the Constitution of the United Kingdom grew up with the gradual development of the free and independent country itself, these other countries are, so to speak, new creations, and have had no time in which to 'evolve' constitutions. But it may be borne in mind that India, Sri Lanka, Ghana, Cyprus, Nigeria, Sierra Leone, Trinidad and Tobago, Uganda, Singapore, Kenya, Tanzania, Malawi, Malta, Nauru, Zambia, the Gambia, Guyana, Botswana, Bangladesh, the Seychelles, Dominica, St Vincent, Kiribati, Zimbabwe, Vanuatu, the Maldives and Mauritius are republics, and have thus renounced allegiance to the Crown, though their constitutions either provide or impliedly recognise that the United Kingdom monarch is to be recognised as symbolic head of the Commonwealth. Lesotho has its Paramount Chief as head of state: Swaziland and Tonga have their own kings, and Brunei has its sultan; and Malaysia and Western Samoa maintain their

---

4   Pakistan, which was a member, left the Commonwealth in 1972.

own special forms of an elected monarchy. Each has therefore renounced allegiance to the Crown, but still recognises the British monarch as the head of the Commonwealth. It is doubtful whether this title means anything in reality. Most independent countries within the Commonwealth have abolished the right of appeal from their courts to the Privy Council. But such a right of appeal still lies from the courts of New Zealand, Fiji, Singapore, Mauritius, the Gambia, Trinidad and Tobago, Jamaica, the Bahamas, Barbados, Dominica, Kiribati, Antigua, Belize, Brunei, St Lucia, St Vincent and Tuvalu.

In a world of growing nationalism the changes in structure and pattern of the Commonwealth come thick and fast; so much so, indeed, that no textbook writer could ever hope to remain up-to-date at the time of publication of his work. The Commonwealth is becoming more and more flexible, and it is clear that any innovation is possible, provided the existing full members are prepared to agree to it. Thus, quite apart from the admission of republics to the Commonwealth, and the diminishing jurisdiction of the Judicial Committee of the Privy Council, one might point, for example, to the admission of Cyprus in 1961, the year after its attainment of independence, for an experimental period of five years—a period which Cyprus itself, after a vote in its House of Representatives, had stipulated in its application to join the Commonwealth, and which has since been prolonged. For the future it is possible that even purely foreign countries, with no former links with the Commonwealth at all, might be admitted, should they apply. Perhaps also the very size of the independent Commonwealth may cause the introduction of some form of regional grouping for certain purposes. The entry of the United Kingdom to the European Community in 1973, mentioned in Chapter 2, might eventually have some effect upon Commonwealth relations and structure, though no significant change has yet become apparent. Some thinkers believe that the Commonwealth is now growing so big that it will cease to be effective for any purpose, save in its common use of the English language and its sharing of the British educational system and parliamentary institutions. Obviously the links between the United Kingdom and the older members, Australia, New Zealand and Canada, must be to some extent closer than those between any of these countries and the other members of the Commonwealth, partly because of blood relationship and partly because the British were never conquerors in the three older countries (except as far as the French Canadians and Maoris were concerned). But there is no sign as yet that the Asian and African members wish to disband the Commonwealth, or even to weaken it appreciably.

An anomalous link between the United Kingdom and Canada remained until 1982. This required certain Canadian constitutional amendments to be passed by the Westminster Parliament, and was included in the Canadian Constitution (the British North America Act 1867) as a kind of check upon undue power being exercised within Canada by any political or ethnic groups against others. The requirement was finally removed, at the request of Canada, by the Canada Act 1982, which provides a new constitution for Canada, and specifically states that no Act of Parliament of the United Kingdom passed thereafter shall extend to Canada as part of its law.

Recent Australian legislation has also effected the abolition of certain similarly anomalous links between the Commonwealth of Australia and the United Kingdom.[5]

In 1965 a Commonwealth Secretariat was established to distribute factual information to member countries, to promote Commonwealth links, and to co-ordinate preparations for meetings of Commonwealth ministers. The first Secretary-General was a Canadian, and his successor, the present Secretary-General, is a QC from Guyana. The Secretariat is based at Marlborough House, London.

III. Other Members of the Commonwealth which are not yet Independent

The so-called Imperialist aims of the nineteenth century have disappeared, and the intentions of all United Kingdom governments in recent years have been to implement as far as possible the almost uniform desire of dependent peoples under

---

5   The military bases over which the United Kingdom has retained sovereignty in the island of Cyprus, and other military agreements with various Commonwealth countries, are in no way legal fetters upon the independence of those countries.

the Crown for self-government. The achievement of this aim must in any case be a comparatively slow process, as some countries are not yet ready to be solely responsible for their own affairs. Furthermore, the aim may not be entirely possible of achievement in the long run for certain small countries which can never be economically self-supporting. It is of great interest to find the recent development of associate status within the Commonwealth, for this may provide the ideal solution for such small countries. The total population of the remaining dependent territories does not exceed six millions, and about five millions of these are in Hong Kong, where there are special reasons why the inhabitants do not at present desire any significant alteration in their colonial status (it may well be that the eventual settlement of Hong Kong will be by some form of joint administration between the People's Republic of China and the United Kingdom).

In this short section we shall merely outline the various types of non-independent countries within the Commonwealth, without attempting to list all the individual territories concerned. The great majority of these countries are subject in some respect to United Kingdom sovereignty, but some are under the control of other independent Commonwealth countries, as has already been mentioned earlier in this chapter. It is not part of our present purpose to relate how the various territories concerned came to have their present status.

A. ASSOCIATE STATES

It will be recalled from Chapter 7 that the Isle of Man and the Channel Islands are not strictly speaking part of the United Kingdom. For practical and international purposes they are grouped together with the United Kingdom as one independent member of the Commonwealth, though they really occupy a position partly independent and partly subordinate to the United Kingdom Parliament. In the second edition of this book it was suggested that this kind of association could be used as a basis for settling the future of small dependencies which could not, for various reasons, contemplate full independence. The settlement of the future of the Leeward and Windward Islands had given particular difficulty, but agreement for a kind of associate status was reached in 1966 and brought into effect by the West Indies Act 1967, which conferred the new status upon Antigua, St Christopher-Nevis-Anguilla and St Lucia. Similar status was gained shortly afterwards by Grenada, Dominica and St Vincent.

Associate states have full control over their internal affairs, and they have the power by constitutional amendment to become fully independent, and thus to end their association with the United Kingdom at any time without further recourse to the United Kingdom government or Parliament. The British government retains responsibility for external affairs and the defence of each state, but otherwise the United Kingdom has no power to legislate for such a state or to conduct its affairs. There is a regional High Court and Court of Appeal for the West Indies.

Most of the West Indian islands which became associate states have now opted for full independent membership of the Commonwealth, and the only remaining associate state now in the Caribbean is Anguilla. But the 1968 Constitution for Gibraltar bears a close resemblance to some of these arrangements.[6] In 1965 the Cook Islands, and in 1974 Niue, became associate states of New Zealand.

B. COLONIES

A colony is any part of the dominions of the Crown which is not yet an independent member of the Commonwealth. The Isle of Man, the Channel Islands and the associate states are, however, excepted from this category. Direct allegiance is owed to the Crown. All persons born in British colonies are British dependent territories citizens. The constitutions of colonies are provided either by Acts of Parliament or, more usually, by Orders in Council or Letters Patent, and the powers and privileges of colonies vary greatly with the local conditions, educational progress etc. Thus a few colonies may still be administered directly from the United Kingdom, but the majority have their own legislative assemblies, of different

---

6 By an exceptional provision in the British Nationality Act 1981 Gibraltarians are eligible for British citizenship, as also by a later statute are those who live in the Falkland Islands.

degrees of representative character, and a few are almost entirely, or even completely, self-governing for internal affairs. All colonies have Governors who represent the Crown. As examples of colonies not yet very advanced in the progress towards self-government may be taken Hong Kong, the Pitcairn Islands, the British Antarctic Territory and St Helena, whereas at the other end of the scale is Bermuda.

C. PROTECTORATES

Protectorates are territories under the protection of the Crown, although they are not strictly British territory or part of the dominions of the Crown. But the Crown is responsible for their foreign affairs. Internally they are administered under British supervision of varying degrees of strictness by their native rulers, or else in a way very similar to those of colonies. The authority for the supervisory powers of the United Kingdom or of any other independent member of the Commonwealth came originally from treaties entered into with the native rulers, but it now derives both from the royal prerogative and from the Foreign Jurisdiction Act 1890. The last British protectorate, the British Solomon Islands, became a full member of the Commonwealth in 1978, but other protectorates might come into existence if wanted.[7]

D. TRUST TERRITORIES

Trust territories (formerly League of Nations mandated territories) are administered by the Crown under the terms of the International Trusteeship system organised by the United Nations. The independent members of the Commonwealth are among a number of countries to which this type of trusteeship has been given. Internally and externally the territories are controlled by the trustee power, but reports must be submitted from time to time to the General Assembly of the United Nations and the Trusteeship Council, which will have an influence over the gradual development of the territories.

---

7 Brunei, which until 1971 held the now obsolete status of a Protected State, then became a sovereign state in treaty relationship with the United Kingdom, which was responsible for the conduct of external affairs, and had a consultative responsibility for defence. But it became fully independent in 1984.

With the independence of Tanganyika in December 1961 the United Kingdom's direct trusteeship responsibilities came to an end, though it is always possible for them to arise again at the behest of the United Nations. Its indirect responsibilities ended with Nauru's independence, granted in 1968. The last trust territory of any kind within the Commonwealth was New Guinea, administered by Australia, which became independent as part of Papua New Guinea in 1975.

IV. The Place of the Commonwealth in British Constitutional Law

There is no attempt in this book to give an account, however short, of the constitutional laws of those countries outside the United Kingdom which are also members in some way of the wider Commonwealth. It may therefore be asked why any mention of the Commonwealth should appear at all in the present volume, which is devoted to the constitutional laws of the United Kingdom. The answer is that British constitutional law is affected by the relationship of the mother country with the other members of the Commonwealth, and therefore it is our final task in this book to indicate briefly the ways in which the law is so affected. This may probably best be done in summary form, in view of the information which has already been given in the foregoing pages of the present chapter.

(1) THE CROWN AND ALLEGIANCE

It used to be thought that the citizens of all independent member states of the Commonwealth must owe allegiance to the Crown, but the existence today of republics within the Commonwealth has disproved this theory. Yet common allegiance to the Crown by all member countries of the Commonwealth, other than the independent republics, Lesotho, Swaziland, Malaysia, Tonga, Western Samoa, protectorates and trust territories, is still an important link, even if the concept of the Crown itself is of a somewhat nebulous quality in this sphere, depending a great deal upon a slightly illogical emotionalism. Even with the republics and the separate monarchies the British monarch remains as the symbol of the unity of the Commonwealth, for those countries recognise him as head of the Commonwealth.

(2) POWER OVER NON-INDEPENDENT MEMBERS OF THE COMMONWEALTH

The considerable power wielded by the United Kingdom or by other independent members of the Commonwealth over most non-independent members is very important for all members, as including an ability to control the destiny of people who are not inhabitants of the British Isles. As has been seen already in Chapters 2, 3, and 10, all such powers stem either from Acts of Parliament or from the royal preorgative.

(3) OTHER LINKS BETWEEN INDEPENDENT MEMBERS OF THE COMMONWEALTH

There are a number of loose links between full members, all of which could be broken at any time by any member acting unilaterally, but it is realised that there is much advantage to be gained from keeping the links. Thus there exist certain reciprocal trading and economic advantages, which are hardly within the scope of this volume. It is customary to enter into agreements with each other of a rather more informal nature than treaties. Conferences of Commonwealth Prime Ministers and Presidents are normally held every two years or so to discuss mutual problems; indeed, consultation at all levels on many subjects probably provides the most important Commonwealth link of all. High Commissioners are usually exchanged by the full members, rather than ambassadors, although their powers and status (as regards diplomatic immunity etc) are similar. The right of appeal from the courts of all member countries to the Judicial Committee of the Privy Council has already been abolished by many independent members, but it still remains for those others which wish to retain it.

The Statute of Westminster 1931, which has been discussed earlier, is particularly important. It expressly applied to, and was later accepted by legislative Acts in, the older independent members of the Commonwealth, and its substantive provisions have been written into the Independence Acts or the constitutions of the post-war independent members. The provisions of the Statute lay down not only the final recognition that all independent members have complete legislative independence for internal and external matters, but also the only way in which the United Kingdom Parliament may still legislate in such a way as to alter the law in any other independent member of the Commonwealth. Section 4 provides: 'No Act of Parliament of the United Kingdom passed after the commencement of this Act shall extend, or be deemed to extend, to a Dominion as part of the law of that Dominion unless it is expressly declared in that Act that the Dominion has requested, and consented to, the enactment thereof'. In view of the strictly sovereign legislative power of the United Kingdom Parliament, discussed above in Chapter 2, it would be possible for this section to be replaced expressly, or even by implication, so far as United Kingdom law *only* is concerned, at any time by another Act passed in the usual way, but, as Lord Sankey LC once said: 'that is theory and has no relation to realities'.[8] It would be unthinkable that any future Parliament should attempt to alter this provision without the requisite 'request' and 'consent'. And in any case, regardless of English law, the law of, say, Australia would not be changed as far as Australia itself was concerned by a United Kingdom Act, unless there had been the requisite 'request' and 'consent'.[9]

(4) THE ADOPTION OF BRITISH INSTITUTIONS

It is noteworthy that the executive, legislative and judicial functions in most full member countries have often followed the model of the United Kingdom, at least in the first instance. There are modifications in all countries, but the basic plan is frequently similar. The modifications may well be quite extensive, and there has been a trend in the African and Asian countries towards a constitution with a presidential system on the United States model, instead of a parliamentary system. But even those Commonwealth countries with this type of constitution have managed to work into their systems many British-type institutions. The transfer of British institutions to other Commonwealth countries may well prove to be the greatest contribution of the United Kingdom to any of these countries. Electoral systems vary, but the parliamentary systems are often similar. Even the much criticised House of Lords is not shunned in all aspects, for where upper Houses have been created their

---

8   *British Coal Corpn v R* [1935] AC 500 at 520, [1935] All ER Rep 139 at 146; and see
    Madzimbamuto v Lardner-Burke [1969] 1 AC 645, [1968] 3 All ER 561.
9   See H. R. Gray 'The Sovereignty of the Imperial Parliament' (1960) 23 MLR 647

membership is usually of a more long term nature than that of the lower House, and in Canada membership of the Senate is for life. Again, it is normal for ministers in all member countries to be members of the legislature, thus following the British pattern of responsibility to Parliament, and eschewing the American type of separation of powers, discussed in Chapter 6.

(5) MEMBERSHIP OF THE HOUSE OF LORDS

Any citizens of independent Commonwealth countries who are also United Kingdom peers, and who wish to sit in the House of Lords in Westminster, may do so. The former Prime Ministers of Australia, Viscount Bruce of Melbourne, and of what was then the Central African Federation of Rhodesia and Nyasaland, Lord Malvern, have done so, though the latter was in any case a native of England. Lord Casey, a former Australian Minister for External Affairs, became a life peer, having been so created under the Life Peerages Act 1958.[10] Though a small matter, it may indicate the elasticity and the strength of the Commonwealth, and the relations between its members.

FURTHER READING

Sir William Dale *The Modern Commonwealth* (1983)
K. C. Wheare *The Constitutional Structure of the Commonwealth* (1960)
The British Commonwealth: The Development of its Laws and Constitutions series 14 Vols
S. A. de Smith *The New Commonwealth and its Constitutions* (1964)
The Annual Survey of Commonwealth Law (13 Vols, 1965–1977)
D. C. M. Yardley 'Commonwealth Membership: its Present and Future' (1960) XIII Parliamentary Affairs 346
A Year Book of the Commonwealth (published annually)

10   See Chapter 2, above.

Index